RETURN TO FLIGHT
Space Shuttle Discovery
PHOTO SCRAPBOOK

Compiled By

DENNIS R. JENKINS and *JORGE R. FRANK*

specialtypress
PUBLISHERS AND WHOLESALERS

ISBN-13 978-1-58007-104-8
ISBN-10 1-58007-104-X

Item Number SP104

39966 Grand Avenue
North Branch, MN 55056 USA
(651) 277-1400 or (800) 895-4585
www.specialtypress.com

Printed in China

Distributed in the UK and Europe by:

Midland Publishing
4 Watling Drive
Hinckley LE10 3EY, England
Tel: 01455 233 747 Fax: 01455 233 737
www.midlandcountiessuperstore.com

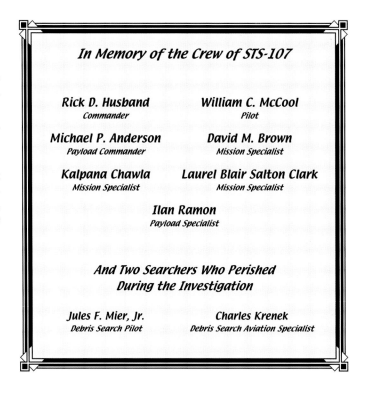

In Memory of the Crew of STS-107

Rick D. Husband
Commander

William C. McCool
Pilot

Michael P. Anderson
Payload Commander

David M. Brown
Mission Specialist

Kalpana Chawla
Mission Specialist

Laurel Blair Salton Clark
Mission Specialist

Ilan Ramon
Payload Specialist

And Two Searchers Who Perished During the Investigation

Jules F. Mier, Jr.
Debris Search Pilot

Charles Krenek
Debris Search Aviation Specialist

On the Cover: **Discovery *docked to the* Destiny *laboratory module at the International Space Station during STS-114. Steve Robinson took this photo during the during the third of three extravehicular activities (EVA) of the mission. Part of the P1 truss and a solar array are visible in the background.* (NASA)**

On the Back Cover (top): **Discovery *as it performed the Rbar Pitch Maneuver. ISS science officer and flight engineer John Phillips used a 400 mm lens for this photo, and the Orbiter was about 600 feet away. ISS commander Sergei Krikalev and Phillips took photos for about 90 seconds as* Discovery *commander Eileen Collins guided the spacecraft through the flip.* (NASA)**

On the Back Cover (bottom): **A wide-angle view of the launch of STS-114 from Launch Complex 39B at the Kennedy Space Center in Florida on 26 July 2005. (NASA)**

On the Title Page: **A wide-angle view of Discovery docked to the ISS with a blue Earth in the background. (NASA)**

On the Contents Page: **The STS-114 crew homecoming at the Johnson Space Center in Houston, Texas. (NASA)**

CONTENTS

INTRODUCTION

On 1 February 2003, the Space Shuttle *Columbia* was coming home from the two-week STS-107 mission. Unrecognized by the crew and those on the ground, *Columbia* had been fatally damaged during ascent on 16 January. A piece of insulating foam – the size of a briefcase and weighing about 1.5 pounds – had come loose from the External Tank (ET) and impacted a Reinforced Carbon-Carbon (RCC) panel on the leading edge of the left wing. The foam opened a breach that allowed 5,000-degree Fahrenheit superheated air into the wing during reentry, leading to structural failure and the loss of *Columbia* and her crew of seven.

Within hours, the Columbia Accident Investigation Board convened. Pending the outcome of the investigation, NASA grounded the Space Shuttle fleet. The accident board released its report in August 2003, calling for changes to hardware, procedures, and management policies.

By late 2004 NASA believed it had solved the problems, and set a launch date of 12 May 2005. The ET had been modified – NASA called it "redesigned" but that was overstating the case – to eliminate the specific piece of foam that had caused the loss of *Columbia* and generally lessen the potential for foam shedding. Nobody knew for sure if the techniques would work since the basic science of why foam shed was not well understood. There would be additional cameras following the vehicle during ascent and the Orbiter Boom Sensor System (OBSS) – an extension for the robotic arm normally carried on the Orbiter – would allow *Discovery* to be checked for damage while on-orbit. There were also sweeping changes to the organizational structure and management policies to preclude the communications problems identified during STS-107.

Further, the Space Shuttle Program decided the first two Return-to-Flight missions would have a "launch on need" rescue vehicle; in the case of STS-114, *Atlantis* stood-by to be stacked as STS-300. With the possible exception of a flight to service the Hubble Space Telescope, all future Space Shuttle missions would head toward the International Space Station that could provide a "safe haven" in case of catastrophic damage. The astronauts would wait on the ISS for the rescue vehicle.

Unfortunately, despite the expenditure of considerable resources, NASA could not develop a viable repair capability for the Orbiter Thermal Protection System. *Discovery* would carry several experimental techniques – a couple would be tested on-orbit – but nobody had much confidence that they could truly repair a stricken Orbiter.

Since it had been over two years since a Space Shuttle had been launched, NASA prudently decided to conduct a "tanking test" at the Kennedy Space Center. This is a full-up countdown, including filling the ET with propellants, but not igniting the engines, that provides a chance to validate all of the hardware is working, as well as giving the launch team a final opportunity to practice. During a test on 14 April, several anomalies were noted with the ET. A second tanking test a couple of weeks later did not instill confidence that the problems were understood, much less solved. It was decided to switch ETs to the one planned for STS-121, and install an additional heater to eliminate ice buildup that had been observed during the tanking tests. This meant that *Discovery* had to be rolled-back from the launch pad, demated from her stack, and moved to the STS-121 stack. It took time.

Finally, on 13 July 2005, all seemed ready. However, during propellant loading, another anomaly was discovered, and the launch attempt was scrubbed. NASA went into troubleshooting mode – both for technical and public relations reasons. In the end, it was decided that the problem was sufficiently well understood to accept flying without fixing it. On 26 July, *Discovery* launched on the first Space Shuttle mission in 30 months. Unrelated to the earlier problems, several anomalies were noted during ascent, including the shedding of pieces of foam large enough to damage the Orbiter. Fortunately, none of this debris impacted *Discovery*. NASA grounded the fleet yet again, pending further investigation. The second Return-to-Flight mission, STS-121, would not launch before May 2006 while more foam was removed from the External Tanks to preclude pieces coming off during ascent.

STS-114 was the most photographed Space Shuttle mission in history. All of the photographs were taken for engineering reasons, not public relations, but are nevertheless, in many cases, spectacular. Most of the photos presented here are of high quality, but a few are less than ideal; they are included because they offer a glimpse of the program that the authors believed was worthy of being seen. The goal was to present an interesting visual record of the mission. We hope you enjoy it.

Dennis R. Jenkins
Cape Canaveral, Florida

Jorge R. Frank
Houston, Texas

RTF-1 ... STS-114

STS-114 was intended to be the 17th flight (ULF1) to the International Space Station (ISS), with a November 2002 launch date. It would have carried the *Raffaello* Multi-Purpose Logistics Module (MPLM) and performed an ISS crew rotation by replacing the Expedition 6 crew of Kenneth Bowersox, Nikolai Budarin, and Donald Pettit with the Expedition 7 crew of Yuri Malenchenko, Aleksandr Kaleri, and Edward Lu. However, the loss of *Columbia* while returning on 1 February 2003 from the STS-107 mission grounded all future Space Shuttle flights.

Instead, the Expedition 6 crew came home in the Soyuz TMA-1 that was already docked at the ISS, being replaced by the two-man crew of Malenchenko and Lu launched aboard Soyuz TMA-2. Resupply was accomplished using the less-capable but perfectly serviceable Russian Progress logistics vehicles.

During the recovery after *Columbia*, STS-114 was manifested as the first Return-to-Flight mission, but the crew rotation task was dropped. The *Raffaello* MPLM was still the primary payload and the mission was now considered a "test flight" to verify modifications made during the stand-down performed as expected. Now, the mission would carry supplies and a new control moment gyro to the ISS, and test various tile and RCC repair techniques on-orbit. Since the Orbiter would no longer be carrying an ISS crew, three additional payload specialists – Charlie Camarda, Wendy Lawrence, and Andy Thomas – were added.

Problems discovered during two tanking tests in April 2005 would further delay the launch while the External Tank was switched with the one intended for STS-121.

The original (left) and revised STS-114 crew patches. Originally, STS-114 was a crew rotation flight, and the names of the International Space Station (ISS) crewmembers that would be transported up and down are on the patch. The revised patch signified the Space Shuttle return-to-flight and honored the memory of the STS-107 Columbia crew. The blue Orbiter rising above Earth's horizon includes the Columba constellation of seven stars, echoing the STS-107 patch and remembers the seven members of that mission. The dominant design element of the revised STS-114 patch is the planet Earth, which represents the unity and dedication of the many people whose efforts allow the Space Shuttle to safely return to flight. Against the background of the Earth at night, the blue orbit represents the International Space Station, with the EVA crewmembers named on the orbit. The red sun on the orbit signifies the contributions of the Japanese Space Agency to the mission and to the ISS program. The multi-colored Space Shuttle plume represents the broad spectrum of challenges for this mission, including Orbiter inspection and repair experiments, and bringing supplies to the ISS. (NASA)

The official crew portrait. In front are James M. Kelly (left), pilot; Wendy B. Lawrence, mission specialist, and Eileen M. Collins (right), commander. In back are mission specialists Stephen K. Robinson (left), Andrew S. W. Thomas, Charles J. Camarda, and Soichi Noguchi.

The STS-114 crew poses in front of Building 2 at the Johnson Space Center, Texas. Each crewmember is dressed in an Advanced Crew Escape Suit (ACES). The series of photos taken during this shoot were used for various Space Flight Awareness posters. (NASA)

Eileen M. Collins

James M. "Vegas" Kelly

Charles J. Camarda

Wendy B. Lawrence

Soichi Noguchi

Stephen K. Robinson

Andrew S. W. Thomas

Relaxing ...

THE TRAINING

At the time of the *Columbia* accident, the STS-114 crew was one month from flight and had nearly completed their training. Unlike the post-Challenger flights, the core of the crew and their mission remained intact during the return-to-flight process. Consequently, this crew received some of the most extensive training in spaceflight history. Repeated flight delays allowed the crew to stretch out their proficiency training in all the standard flight phases, while adding new training for return-to-flight tasks such as Orbiter inspection and repair. As with all other Space Shuttle flights, most of the training occurred at the Johnson Space Center (JSC), although a substantial amount was conducted at other NASA centers and contractor facilities.

Like all Space Shuttle crews, the members of STS-114 practiced how to evacuate an Orbiter if necessary using the Full Fuselage Trainer (FFT) at the Space Vehicle Mockup Facility in Building 9NW at the Johnson Space Center. The slides are very similar to those used on commercial airliners, while the rope is a common technique used to escape from the cockpit of most large aircraft. (NASA)

Crews receive Water Survival Training at the Sonny Carter Training Facility at JSC (also known as the Neutral Buoyancy Laboratory – NBL). James Kelly (left photo) and Eileen Collins (center photo) are shown in their rafts. At right, Steve Robinson is shown being lifted out of the water, as would happen during a helicopter rescue. All the astronauts are attired in training versions of the Advanced Crew Escape Suits used on the Space Shuttle. In 1995 the new NBL, near Ellington Field, was named in honor of the late astronaut M. L. "Sonny" Carter, who was instrumental in developing many of the current space-walking techniques used by the astronauts. (NASA)

One of the "fun" parts of training are flights in the Northrop T-38 Talon jet trainers out of Ellington Field near JSC. This is Eileen Collins doing a preflight inspection (NASA)

The astronauts fly aboard the NASA KC-135 "Vomit Comet" that simulates a weightless environment. Among other things, the astronauts learned to repair tiles while in a simulated environment. Aboard this particular flight were "Stevie Ray" Robinson, Charlie Camarda, and Soichi Noguchi. The KC-135 has since been replaced by a surplus military C-9. (NASA)

Other training includes how to use the escape pole that telescopes out of the crew hatch and allows astronauts to bail out while the Orbiter is in subsonic level flight. This is basic training with a stub pole. (NASA)

The Shuttle Mission Simulator (SMS) consists of two fixed-base simulators for on-orbit training, and a motion-base simulator for ascent/entry training. This is the instructor station during an on-orbit simulation. (NASA)

The Sonny Carter Training Facility has extensive classroom facilities. Here the STS-114 crew listens to an instructor in one of the classrooms. Note the closed-circuit television monitors along the back wall. (NASA)

In one of the cockpits at the Space Vehicle Mockup Facility, James Kelly is in the pilot's seat while mission specialists Steve Robinson and Andy Thomas look on. The mockups in the facility range from simple procedure trainers to complex replicas of the Orbiter that duplicate every switch and display. (NASA)

Seen during February 2005, Charlie Camarda (left), Wendy Lawrence, and Soichi Noguchi, are seated on the mid-deck of one of the high fidelity trainers in the Space Vehicle Mockup Facility for an emergency egress training session. All are attired in training versions of the Advanced Crew Escape Suits. (NASA)

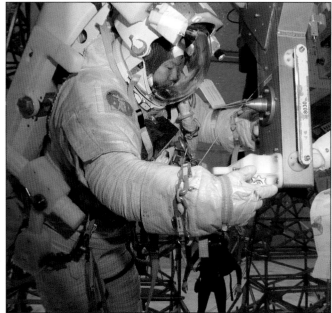

Soichi Noguchi wears a training version of the Extravehicular Mobility Unit (EMU) spacesuit during an underwater EVA simulation at the Neutral Buoyancy Laboratory. Steve Robinson, the other mission specialist scheduled to make spacewalks during STS-114, was out of the frame. Noguchi represents Japan's Aerospace Exploration Agency (JAXA), formerly the National Space Development Agency (NASDA). (NASA)

Charlie Camarda checks data on a monitor in the aft section of the cabin of the fixed-base Shuttle Mission Simulator at the Mission Simulation and Training Facility. The rehearsal was part of a long-duration integrated simulation for STS-114. The two rear windows on the Orbiter look into the payload bay. (NASA)

Wendy Lawrence and James Kelly perform a communications check in a mockup of the International Space Station's Destiny laboratory module in the Space Vehicle Mockup Facility in July 2005. This photo was taken from the aft end of the module looking forward. (NASA)

NASA has a name for everything, and these photos were taken in the Thermal Protection System Trainer, where on-orbit repair techniques can be evaluated and practiced. Here Charlie Camarda looks over one of the plugs designed to repair a hole in the Reinforced Carbon-Carbon panels on the wing leading edge. The plug is held into place against the RCC panel with a toggle bolt made from a superalloy called TZM (titanium, zirconium, and molybdenum). This technique is considered promising, but was not tested on STS-114. NASA has manufactured a dozen different plug shapes to conform to the various curvatures on the RCC panels. The plug can patch a hole up to 4 inches in diameter. (NASA)

VEHICLE PROCESSING

Initially, NASA believed it could begin flying again relatively soon after the accident. Several dates were set in late 2003, only to be missed as the accident board took longer than expected to reach their conclusions. The first date set after the release of the accident report was 12 September 2004, using OV-104, *Atlantis*.

However, correcting the problems identified by the accident board proved harder than expected, and it was soon obvious to all involved that truly correcting the underlying cause of the accident – foam shedding from the External Tank – would take a while. Maintenance and modifications of OV-103, *Discovery*, proceeded faster than expected, and a decision was made to switch Orbiters for STS-114. *Atlantis* was out; *Discovery* was in.

As the launch of STS-114 continued to slip, the Solid Rocket Boosters (SRB) and External Tank (ET) originally stacked for the mission in late 2002 were unstacked, and the SRBs were sent back to the manufacturer to be test fired since they had exceeded their five-year shelf-life; the test was nominal.

Unusually, problems with the External Tank (ET-120) discovered during a pair of tanking tests in April 2005 forced NASA to roll-back from the pad so that *Discovery* could be demated and switched to the stack (using ET-121) originally intended for the second Return-to-Flight mission, STS-121.

This is how Discovery (OV-103) looked in August 2002 when it was rolled over from the Vehicle Assembly Building (VAB) to one of the Orbiter Processing Facility (OPF) High Bays to undergo major maintenance and modifications. The Forward Reaction Control System (FRCS) pod, and both Orbital Maneuvering System (OMS) pods are missing, as are several pieces of Reinforced Carbon-Carbon (RCC) from the leading edge of the wing. RCC was developed by Vought in Grand Prairie, Texas, and is used on areas of the Orbiter where entry temperatures exceed 2,300 degrees Fahrenheit. This was a normally-scheduled Orbiter Major Modification (OMM) period before the loss of Columbia. (NASA)

After the loss of Columbia, it was expected that Atlantis (OV-104) would be the first Orbiter to fly again. Here, Atlantis is being prepared to be towed from the OPF to the VAB in December 2003. The move was necessary to allow annual maintenance on the OPF, which cannot be accomplished with an Orbiter inside. Work in the processing facility included annual validation of the cranes, work platforms, lifting mechanisms, and jack stands. Atlantis remained in the VAB for 10 days, then returned to the OPF to continue processing toward the launch of STS-114. The photo at left shows the missing nose cap and FRCS pod, and most of the wing leading edge RCC panels have also been removed. The wide-angle shot at right shows that all three Space Shuttle Main Engines (SSME) are missing, although the two OMS pods are installed on either side of the vertical stabilizer. Note the body flap in its drooped position. (NASA)

Atlantis during the short trip from the OPF to the VAB. The Orbiter is towed over normal roads between the facilities. OV-104 was the Orbiter that was most-flight-ready, with mostly normal maintenance tasks remaining (excepting reinstalling the RCC panels that had been removed for testing after the loss of Columbia). At this point, STS-114 was tentatively scheduled for September 2004. (NASA)

On 16 December 2003, Atlantis rolled out of the VAB, heading back to the OPF. No major work was performed on the Orbiter while it was in the VAB. Note the "tent" in the VAB Transfer Aisle that protected the Orbiter from anything dropping from above. As the launch date for STS-114 moved out it started becoming clear that OV-103 was going to be selected for the mission. (NASA)

After the Columbia accident, additional insulation was added between the RCC panels (right) and the wing leading edge spar. This will help protect the spar if there is a small hole in the RCC panel, but will not prevent an accident like Columbia. (NASA)

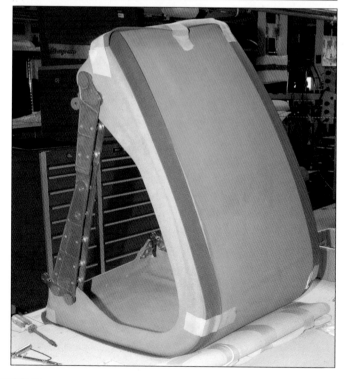

Technicians replace the attachment points for the spars on the interior of a wing of Atlantis (above). The RCC panels (right) are mechanically attached to the wing with a series of floating joints to reduce loading on the panels caused by wing deflections. (NASA)

Segments of a Reusable Solid Rocket Motor (RSRM) are shipped to the Kennedy Space Center (KSC) from the ATK Thiokol plant in Utah via rail. Each of these rail cars holds a single segment. In this case, these particular segments are returning to Utah to be test fired. The segments had been part of the original STS-114 stack in early 2004 and had exceeded their design life of five years, so NASA wanted to test them to collect aging data. (NASA)

An RSRM segment on its transportation cradle in the Rotation Processing and Surge Facility (RPSF) at KSC. The domed end identifies this as the uppermost (forward) segment on an SRB. (NASA)

An SRB aft skirt and lower segment leaves the Rotation Processing and Surge Facility (RPSF). The segments are transported to the VAB where they are stacked on a Mobile Launch Platform (MLP). (NASA)

Inside the VAB, the right aft center SRB segment is prepared for lifting onto the lower segment that is already on the MLP. The assembled SRBs are 149.16 feet high and 12.17 feet in diameter. (NASA)

The segment will be lifted 16 floors in the VAB Transfer Aisle before being moved into the High Bay where the stack is assembled. Each SRB generates a peak thrust of about 3.1 million pounds (lbf). (NASA)

Employees in the Assembly and Refurbishment Facility (ARF) on the Cape Canaveral Air Force Station (CCAFS) sign a banner recognizing their efforts in preparing the first SRB aft skirt for STS-114. The segment is towed to the RPSF where an aft motor segment and an External Tank attach ring are installed. The assembly will then be moved to the VAB and placed on an MLP as the first part of stacking the vehicle. (NASA)

The segments are connected to each other at "field joints" using 177 pins. Note the hole in the center of the segment; the solid propellant burns from inside out along its entire length (NASA)

A Solid Rocket Booster (SRB) is made up of four RSRM segments, plus an aft skirt, nose cap, frustrum, and forward skirt. The nose cap contains the pilot and drogue parachutes while the main parachutes are packed in the frustrum. The SRBs provide most of the thrust to lift the Space Shuttle off the pad and ascend to 150,000 feet, where they are jettisoned two minutes after liftoff. The boosters are recovered in the Atlantic, approximately 141 miles downrange. The External Tank (ET) is attached to each SRB at the bottom of the forward skirt – this is the only load-bearing attachment between the SRB and ET (the bottom attachment point is a non-load-bearing sway brace). (NASA)

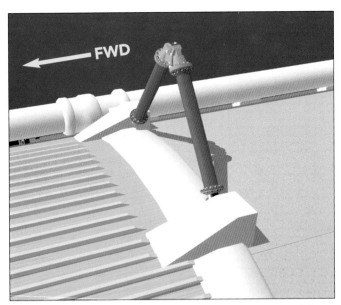

The technical cause of the Columbia accident was the loss of the –Y (left) bipod ramp – the white ramp in the lower center of this computer illustration. The ramps were originally installed to prevent ice buildup on the bipod fitting since it is in close proximity to the liquid hydrogen tank. The bipod connects the ET to the Orbiter. (NASA)

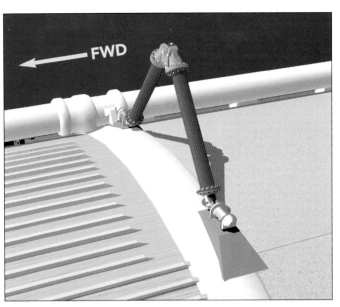

The bipod ramps had been 30 inches long, 14 inches wide, and 12 inches tall. They were sprayed by hand using BX250 or BX265 foam. After the loss of Columbia, the ramps were eliminated completely and electrical heaters installed around the bipod to prevent ice from forming in the humid Florida launch environment. (NASA)

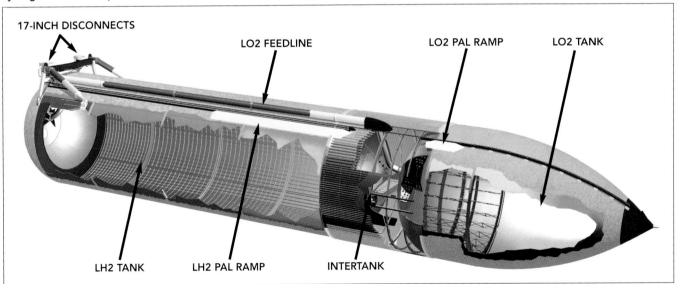

The External Tank (ET) is the only disposable element of the Space Shuttle. The liquid oxygen (LO2) and liquid hydrogen (LH2) propellants for the Space Shuttle Main Engines are carried in the LO2 tank at top and the LH2 tank at bottom. A structural intertank connects the two. A large liquid oxygen feedline runs along the outside of the tank to carry the LO2 to the 17-inch disconnects at the bottom that connect to the Orbiter. Various electrical cables and gaseous pressurization lines run alongside the feedline. (NASA)

The External Tank is manufactured by Lockheed Martin at the Michoud Assembly Facility near New Orleans. This plant was originally built to manufacture Army tanks during World War II, and later built stages for the Saturn launch vehicle (lower right). (NASA)

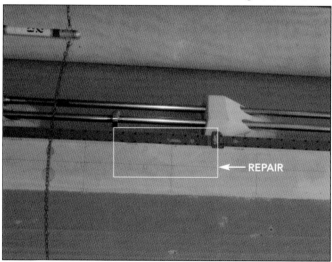

← REPAIR

A photo taken during the assembly of ET-121, the tank ultimately used for the STS-114 Return-to-Flight mission. A lighter-colored area on the LH2 protuberance air load (PAL) ramp, just to the left and below of the ice-frost ramp that has two pressurization lines running through it, shows the location of a repair made during manufacture. This repair failed during ascent and shed a large piece of debris (see page 37). (NASA)

A liquid oxygen tank during assembly. The two propellant tanks form the outer mold line of the ET, which is why foam insulation has to be installed on the outside of the ET. (NASA)

Liquid hydrogen requires a large storage space since it is very light, and the two technicians give scale to an LH2 tank. The current Super Light Weight Tanks (SLWT) are constructed from an aluminum-lithium alloy that allows the Space Shuttle to carry more payload. (NASA)

A tugboat maneuvers the Pegasus barge carrying an External Tank to the dock at the Launch Complex 39 Turn Basin at KSC. For the 900-mile trip between Michoud and Cape Canaveral the barge is towed by one of the SRB retrieval ships – Freedom Star or Liberty Star – before turning the barge over to local tugboats for the final trip to LC-39. The Turn Basin was originally constructed to receive stages of the Saturn launch vehicle during the Apollo moon program in the 1960s. (NASA)

There is a dock at the Turn Basin where the Pegasus can unload the ETs for the short trip to the VAB. The ET is loaded onto its special transport trailer at Michoud and stays on it until it arrives in the VAB. Because the Columbia accident was traced to foam shedding from the ET, NASA and contractor Lockheed Martin developed changes to the tank to prevent large pieces of foam from coming off. This necessitated that the ETs already delivered to KSC before the accident be returned to Michoud for modification. The photos above actually show ET-118 being loaded onto the barge in October 2004 for the trip back to Michoud, but deliveries look exactly the same. (NASA)

ET-121 being delivered to KSC on 6 January 2005. The VAB shows the damage caused by Hurricane Frances during the Labor Day weekend of 2004. Lockheed Martin made numerous changes to the design and application of the foam insulation on the ET after the Columbia accident. The foam is necessary to keep the cryogenic propellants inside the tank cold, prevent ice formation before launch, and protect the ET from ascent heating. (NASA)

The ET is moved, still on its transporter, into the VAB Transfer Aisle before being lifted into an ET checkout cell in High Bay 3. KSC usually has several ETs on hand to support the expected launch manifest. (NASA)

The ET being raised off its transporter in the Transfer Aisle and lifted into a checkout cell in High Bay 3 where the mechanical, electrical, and thermal protection systems are inspected. The ET is 153.8 feet long and 27.6 feet in diameter. A 49.33-foot-long, 143,351-gallon liquid oxygen tank is located forward and a 96.66-foot-long, 385,265-gallon liquid hydrogen tank is aft. These propellants are used by the three Space Shuttle Main Engines to accelerate the Orbiter to approximately 17,500 mph during the first 8.5 minutes of ascent. (NASA)

The Space Shuttle Main Engines (SSME) are shipped to KSC by road in special containers (far left). Inside the SSME Processing Facility at KSC, technicians remove the engine from its container (left). This engine is returning from the Stennis Space Center in Mississippi where it underwent a hot fire acceptance test. Typically, the SSMEs are installed on an Orbiter in the OPF approximately five months before launch. (NASA)

The large nozzles on the SSME are 113 inches long and the outside diameter at the exit is 94 inches. The inner surface of the combustion chamber and the inner surface of the nozzle are cooled by gaseous hydrogen flowing through 1,080 coolant passages. Each Block II SSME generates 393,800-lbf at sea level and 488,800-lbf in a vacuum at 104.5-percent power. (NASA)

The first SSME was installed in Discovery during December 2004. The base heat shield around the bottom of the engine has not been installed yet. STS-114 used engines #2057 (position 1), #2054 (position 2), and #2056 (position 3). Each of these engines is the latest Block II standard using Pratt & Whitney turbopumps. (NASA)

The second SSME was installed in position 3. Note the protective cover on the body flap beneath the main engines and around the OMS pod above the engine. Each SSME burns 1,035 pounds of propellant (889 pounds of LO2 and 146 pounds of LH2) per second. These are the most complex rocket engines ever built. (NASA)

The third SSME being installed in Discovery for STS-114. The original Rocketdyne turbopumps proved to be maintenance intensive and were replaced during the mid-1990s. The Pratt & Whitney turbopumps that feed the propellants into the combustion chamber operate at 23,700 rpm and generate 25,580 shaft horsepower. (NASA)

All three SSMEs are installed in Discovery, although the base heat shields and final Thermal Protection System closeouts are still missing. The two smaller Orbital Maneuvering System (OMS) engines are covered by red nozzle covers. Note the extensive series of work stands around the Orbiter in the OPF. (NASA)

The Orbital Maneuvering System (OMS) pods contain the OMS engines and the aft Reaction Control System (RCS) thrusters. Each pod is 21.8 feet long, 11.37 feet wide at its aft end, and 8.41 feet wide at the forward end. Each OMS engine produces 6,000-lbf in a vacuum and is used for the final boost to orbit and also for deorbit at the end of mission. The engines use hypergolic nitrogen tetroxide (N2O4) and monomethyl hydrazine (MMH) which do not require an ignition system. The aft RCS uses 12 primary thrusters and 2 vernier thrusters per pod, burning the same N2O4 and MMH propellants as the OMS engines. STS-114 used pods LP01 (originally delivered with Challenger, OV-099) and RP03 (originally delivered with Discovery, OV-103). (NASA)

The Forward Reaction Control System (FRCS) is located in the extreme nose of the Orbiter and provides the thrust for attitude (rotational) maneuvers (pitch, yaw, and roll) and for small velocity changes along the Orbiter axes (translation maneuvers). The FRCS contains 14 primary and 2 vernier thrusters that use N2O4 and MMH propellants. The primary thrusters provide 870-lbf in a vacuum and the vernier thrusters produce 24-lbf. STS-114 used FRC3 that had been delivered with Discovery. (NASA)

Water is released onto a Mobile Launch Platform (MLP) on Launch Pad 39A at the start of a sound suppression water test. Workers and the media are on hand to witness the unusual event. This test was conducted following the replacement of the six main system valves, which had been in place since the beginning of the Space Shuttle Program and had reached the end of their service life. The sound suppression water system is installed on the launch pads to protect the Orbiter and its payloads from damage by acoustical energy reflected from the MLP during launch. The system includes an elevated 300,000-gallon water tank that is 290 feet high and stands on the northeast side of each launch pad. The water is released just before the ignition of the SRBs, and flows through parallel 7-foot-diameter pipes onto the MLP. (NASA)

Hurricane Frances hit KSC and Cape Canaveral during the Labor Day weekend of 2004. Numerous panels were blown off the VAB, and there was extensive damage to the Processing Control Center (PCC) that houses offices and a computer center. The Launch Control Center escaped serious damage, as did the launch pads. (NASA)

Considerable damage was sustained by the second floor of the Thermal Protection System Facility from Hurricane Frances. This is the facility where tiles and blankets for the Orbiter TPS were manufactured. The building was considered a total loss and was replaced by a new facility in late 2005. (NASA)

For a while, it seemed that everything that could go wrong was going wrong. One example was the rudder/speedbrake actuators (right). These actuators move the split rudder/speedbrake that is used for control during entry. During Discovery's 2002–2003 OMM, engineers found corrosion on the actuators which were replaced with four spares from inventory. Further inspection revealed that, at least in one case, a gear had been installed upside down. Corrosion on similar actuators that control the body flap led engineers to inspect the same parts on the rudder/speedbrake. The other two Orbiters were also inspected and repaired. (NASA)

NASA's two high-altitude WB-57F aircraft were modified to carry large telescopes in their noses to photograph the Space Shuttle during ascent and descent. The WB-57 Ascent Video Experiment (WAVE) used a 32-inch-ball turret that housed both HDTV and infrared cameras attached to a 11-inch-diameter, 4.2 meter fixed-focal-length lens. During launch, the airplanes flew from Patrick AFB. Unfortunately, WAVE produced video of less than stellar quality. (NASA)

Additional cameras were installed around the launch site as part of the Return-to-Flight effort. These include ten Contraves-Goerz Kineto Tracking Mounts (KTM). The KTM is designed for remote-controlled operations and offers film and digital cameras configured with 20-inch to 150-inch focal length lenses. The long-range tracking cameras located around central Florida were also upgraded, eliminating problems identified during the accident investigation. (NASA)

Another part of the Return-to-Flight effort was the installation of a digital still camera in the right-hand liquid oxygen umbilical well on each Orbiter. This camera provides high-resolution images of the ET following separation of the ET from the Orbiter. See page 34 for a sample of the images from this camera. Previously, the two umbilical cameras (still and motion) had used film that could not be processed until after the Orbiter landed. (NASA)

The Multi-Purpose Logistics Module (MPLM) called Raffaello is shown in the Space Station Processing Facility at KSC. The MPLMs were built by the Italian Space Agency to serve as reusable logistics carriers and are the primary delivery system to resupply and return cargo requiring a pressurized environment to and from the International Space Station. (NASA)

This photo shows all three MPLMs (two at right and one at the back on the left) on the floor of the Space Station Processing Facility in February 2004. This was the first time all three – Leonardo, Raffaello, and Donatello – had been in one location. (NASA)

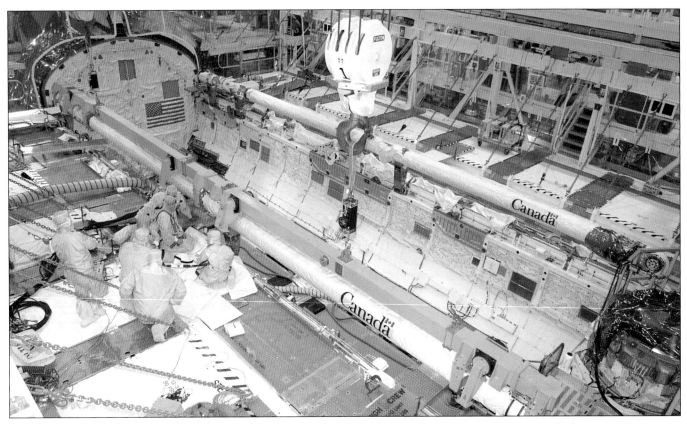

Workers install the Orbiter Boom Sensor System (OBSS, foreground) on the starboard sill of the payload bay. The 50-foot-long OBSS attaches to the Shuttle Remote Manipulator System (RMS, background). Sensors mounted on the end of the OBSS will allow the crew to inspect virtually the entire surface of the Orbiter Thermal protection System on-orbit. Unlike the RMS, which has six joints, the OBSS is a fixed structure. The OBSS was made using spare parts that had been manufactured for the RMS arms. (NASA)

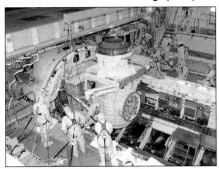

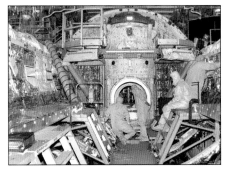

Technicians in the OPF help guide the Orbiter Docking System (ODS) as a crane lowers it into Discovery's payload bay for installation. The airlock is sized to accommodate two fully suited crewmembers simultaneously. In addition to mating to the ISS, the airlock supports depressurization and repressurization, extravehicular activity equipment recharge, liquid-cooled garment water cooling, EVA equipment checkout, and communications. (NASA)

Workers check paperwork about the wiring being installed in Discovery's payload bay that will support the OBSS. Note the variety of workstands and platforms in the payload bay before the cargo is installed. (NASA)

Discovery is lifted vertically by an overhead crane in the Transfer Aisle of the VAB. Note the large cradle that fits around the Orbiter and is attached to points in the structure that makes up the forward and aft payload bay bulkheads. The Orbiter will be lifted up 16 floors and into a High Bay where it will be lowered into place and mated to a waiting ET/SRB stack. (NASA)

Various views of Discovery after it was mated to the ET/SRB stack on top of an MLP. Note the work platforms that allow access to every area of the stack. In the middle photo, the small black fairing on the ET just to the right of the Orbiter's nose covers the top of the liquid oxygen feedline that carries LO2 from the ET to the SSMEs. This fairing also contained a small video camera that provided fascinating images of the vehicle during ascent. The FRCS thrusters are covered with Tyvek™ to keep water out of them while the vehicle is on the pad. Prior to STS-114 they had been covered with plain butcher paper, but NASA worried this could damage the TPS as it came off during ascent. (NASA)

Framed in the open doors of the VAB, Discovery meets the light of day as it begins its slow journey to Launch Pad 39B. First motion was at 2:04 p.m. EDT on 6 April 2005. The Crawler-Transporter underneath the MLP is 20 feet high, 131 feet long, 114 feet wide, and moves at a maximum of one mile per hour. (NASA)

The view from inside the Launch Control Center (LCC) as the STS-114 stack moves toward the launch pad. The LCC is located alongside the VAB, and is approximately three miles from the launch pads – this was deemed a safe distance during the Apollo program in case a vehicle exploded on the pad. (NASA)

The Space Shuttle follows the same rock-covered roadbed created for the Apollo moon program in the 1960s. The entire stack weighs approximately 3 million pounds and would crush any paved surface. Launch Complex 39A is in the background. (NASA)

Aboard the International Space Station, Expedition 10 Commander Leroy Chiao used a digital camera on 6 April to photograph the roll-out of Discovery from an altitude of 220 statute miles. The arrow shows the location of the stack on its way to LC-39B on the far left of the photo. LC-39A is near the beach in the center. (NASA)

An optimistic banner. Discovery being prepared to roll back to the VAB to swap ETs after anomalies during two tanking tests forced the program to change from ET-120 to ET-121. Among other changes, a heater was installed on the LO2 feedline to prevent the formation of ice while loading the ET. (NASA)

Discovery being demated from its stack in VAB High Bay 1. The Orbiter would be placed in the Transfer Aisle before being mated with a different ET. The launch windows for STS-114 were very precise, mainly to ensure that launch and ET separation occurred in daylight so that they could be photographed for engineering analysis. After the roll-back to swap ETs, the new launch window extended from 13 July to 31 July, 2005. (NASA)

Each Orbiter carries its name and the American Flag on the starboard wing. The markings are painted over the Nomex felt reusable surface insulation (FRSI) used on the top of the wing. (NASA)

Viewed from behind, Discovery rests on a transporter in the Transfer Aisle of the VAB. The Orbiter was demated from its ET/SRB stack in High Bay 1 and later moved to High Bay 3 for mating with the ET/SRB stack originally intended for STS-121. (NASA)

The VAB is equipped with a series of cranes capable of lifting heavy loads very precisely. Here a worker attaches the 175-ton bridge crane to Discovery in preparation for lifting the Orbiter up and into High Bay 3 to mate with her new ET/SRB stack. (NASA)

FINALLY, LAUNCH

After switching stacks, *Discovery* was rolled back out to LC-39B for a launch attempt on 13 July 2005. Many engineers questioned why the program had decided not to conduct a tanking test prior to committing to launch, mainly in order to verify whether the problems discovered earlier had indeed been fixed. However, management concluded that a tanking test was not needed, mainly to save the costs associated with it.

Ironically, the launch attempt on 13 July uncovered exactly the problems engineers had been concerned about, and the launch was scrubbed. A tremendous troubleshooting effort followed. Eventually NASA decided that the problems were sufficiently well understood to proceed with the launch. At 10:39 a.m. on 26 July 2005, *Discovery* lifted off from LC-39B headed for the International Space Station.

The STS-114 crew sits for the traditional launch day breakfast in the Operations and Checkout (O&C) building. From the left are Wendy Lawrence, James Kelly, Soichi Noguchi, Eileen Collins, Andy Thomas, Steve Robinson, and Charlie Camarda. (NASA)

Dawn breaks over the Atlantic Ocean as members of the press wait for the launch of STS-114. Various hospitality areas had been set up to accommodate the reporters and invited guests. Weather was typical for Florida in July – hot and humid. (NASA)

The crew exits the O&C building for their ride to LC-39B. On the left, front to back, are James Kelly, Wendy Lawrence, Charlie Camarda, and Andy Thomas. On the right are Eileen Collins, Soichi Noguchi, and Steve Robinson. (NASA)

Members of the engineering team met in the LCC to troubleshoot a LH2 tank low-level fuel cut-off sensor. The sensor failed a routine prelaunch check during the launch countdown on 13 July, causing managers to scrub the first launch attempt. (NASA)

The countdown clock at the press site at Launch Complex 39. The clock shows hours, minutes, and seconds until launch. Thousands of journalists, photographers, and television reporters were on hand for the launch of STS-114. (NASA)

Discovery lifts off at 10:39 a.m. EDT, 26 July 2005, on the STS-114 Return-to-Flight mission. This was the 114th Space Shuttle flight and the 31st for Discovery. The 12-day mission was expected to end at the KSC Shuttle Landing Facility on 7 August. (NASA)

The SRBs are jettisoned two minutes into flight, and the 165,000-pound cases splash down in the Atlantic at about 62 mph. The spent SRBs are retrieved by two recovery vessels and returned for refurbishment and eventual reuse on future Space Shuttle flights. Although several studies have shown there is no particular cost savings from retrieving the spent SRBs, it allows engineers to assess their post-flight condition to ensure anomalies similar to what doomed Challenger in 1986 are not repeated. In these photos, the Freedom Star recovers a spent SRB from the STS-114 launch on July 26. Divers retrieve the cases and the ships tow them back to port. Once at Hangar AF at Cape Canaveral Air Force Station, mobile gantry cranes lift the SRBs onto tracked dollies where they are safed and the cases refurbished. The empty cases are then sent by rail to ATK Thiokol in Utah to be refilled with propellant. (NASA)

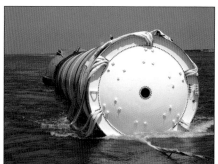

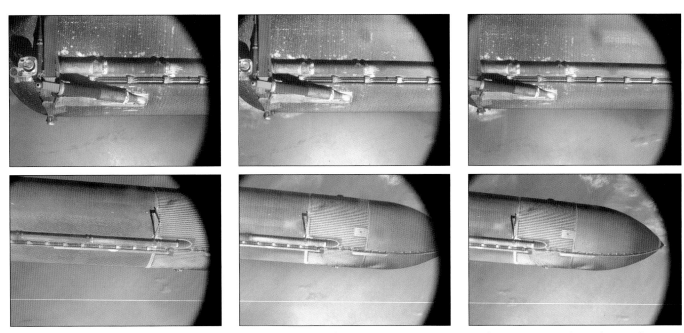

Digital still images from the liquid oxygen umbilical well camera showing ET-121 as it separates from Discovery. Several anomalies were noted from these images and ones taken from a hand held camera in the crew compartment. (NASA)

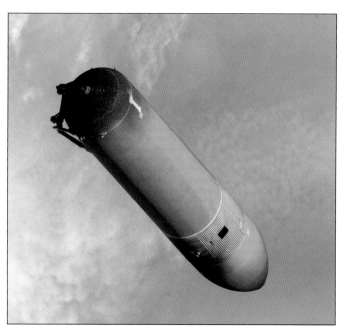

Sequence of images taken by the crew of STS-114. The aft end of the ET is charred from the SRB and SSME exhaust during ascent. The nose is blackened from aerodynamic heating, while the black marks on the side of the tank are from the forward SRB separation motors. (NASA)

In order for the crew to photograph the ET it is necessary to pitch the Orbiter upside down shortly after separation; this maneuver was performed sooner than usual to ensure a good view of the tank. The ET eventually burns up during entry and does not impact land. (NASA)

  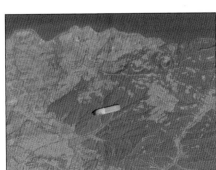

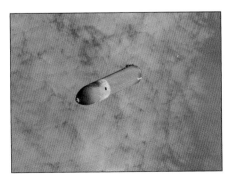 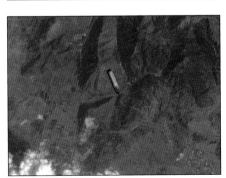

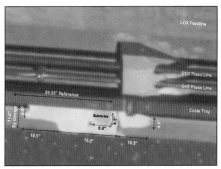

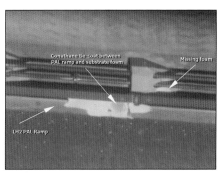

Analysts at the Marshall Space Flight Center pored over the images of the ET downlinked while Discovery was on-orbit. At top left is a frame showing the two major areas of concern – a divot just ahead of the ET bipod (exactly where the bipod ramp had been that caused the Columbia accident) and a large piece of the LH2 protuberance air load (PAL) ramp. Compare the damage to the repair on page 17. The other two frames at top show dimensions and other details about the missing portion of the PAL ramp. At left is a dimensioned photo of the divot ahead of the bipod. This area had been extensively modified after the STS-107 accident to eliminate the bipod ramp that doomed Columbia. In addition, a heater was added to eliminate ice formation around the bipod. At lower right is a dimensioned photo of foam missing around an ice/frost ramp further aft on the ET (it shows up in the middle three photos on page 34). (NASA)

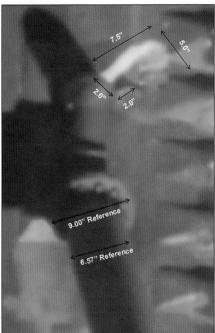

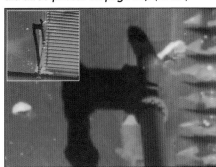

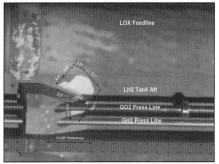

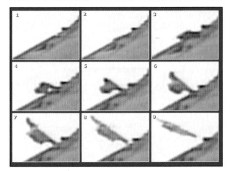

Views from the camera mounted in the LO2 feedline fairing near the top of the ET. At left are nine frames showing the LH2 PAL ramp separating from ET-121 during ascent; the piece was large enough to cause catastrophic damage to the Orbiter Thermal Protection System, but fortunately, it did not hit the Orbiter. The other two frames show the right SRB at separation. (NASA)

APPROACHING THE ISS

During the launch of STS-114, engineers observed several pieces of insulating foam come off the External Tank on real-time video of the launch (see page 37). This was not altogether unexpected since nobody had ever watched the Space Shuttle during ascent with as many cameras as were trained on STS-114. Nevertheless, the apparent foam shedding added new emphasis on the Rbar Pitch Maneuver (RPM) that would be performed as *Discovery* approached the ISS (see page 40), as well as the self-examination to be performed using the Orbiter Boom Sensor System attached to *Discovery*'s robotic arm. Between these two procedures, STS-114 would become the most photographed Space Shuttle mission yet.

Discovery's open payload bay seen from the aft flight deck window. The Orbiter Docking System (ODS) is visible in the foreground and the External Stowage Platform 2 and Raffaello Multi-Purpose Logistics Module are behind it. (NASA)

Views of the ISS taken as Discovery approached. In all photos the ISS coordinate system is: aft is left, forward is right, port is down, starboard is up, nadir is "out of the page," and zenith is "into the page." Several ISS details should be noted, including the cluster of nadir windows on the Zvezda module (from which the RPM photos were taken), the pair of Soyuz docking targets on the nadir side of Pirs, and the various clusters of black-and-white dots scattered over the US modules, which are used as targets for the Canadian Space Vision System (SVS). (NASA)

A Russian Progress supply vehicle (left) docked to the aft ($-X_A$) side of the Russian Zvezda service module. Progress is used to bring supplies, including water, to the ISS. (NASA)

Left to right: Zvezda, the Pirs docking compartment docked to the nadir ($+Z_A$) side of Zvezda, Zarya functional cargo block docked to the forward ($+X_A$) side of Zvezda. (NASA)

Left to right: Zarya, a Soyuz (aft end toward camera) docked to the nadir side of Zarya, Pressurized Mating Adapter (PMA) 1 and Unity node docked to the forward side of Zarya, Quest joint airlock berthed to the starboard ($+Y_A$) side of Unity, PMA-3 berthed to the Port ($-Y_A$) side of Unity, and the Destiny laboratory berthed to the forward side of Unity. (NASA)

RBAR PITCH MANEUVER

A major objective of STS-114 was to completely survey the Orbiter Thermal Protection System as soon as the vehicle was on-orbit. In addition to a self-survey using the Orbiter Boom Sensor System, the crew of the ISS would photograph every inch of the Orbiter from the Zvezda module.

As *Discovery* approached within 2,000 feet below and behind the ISS, Eileen Collins began manually flying the Orbiter toward the Rbar, or radial vector toward the station, the imaginary line drawn between the ISS and the Earth. She slowed *Discovery*'s approach and flew to a point about 600 feet directly below the station. On a verbal cue from James Kelly, Collins commanded *Discovery* into a nose-forward, three-quarter-of-a-degree-per-second backflip. As the Orbiter passed 145 degrees into the maneuver, Vegas told Sergei Krikalev and John Phillips to begin their photography of the Orbiter. The station crew used windows 6 and 7 in the Zvezda service module to shoot with Kodak DCS 760 digital cameras equipped with 400mm (Phillips) and 800mm (Krikalev) lenses.

The digital camera with the 400mm lens was used to capture imagery of the upper surfaces of the Orbiter with a two-inch resolution. The other camera with the 800mm lens was used to concentrate on the underside, capturing pictures of the nose landing gear door seals, the main landing gear door seals, and the elevon cove with one-inch analytical resolution. There was sufficient time during the 90-second backflip time for two sets of pictures.

At the end of the maneuver, *Discovery* was oriented with its payload bay facing the station. Collins then moved the Orbiter to a point about 400 feet in front of the ISS along the direction of travel for both spacecraft, known as the Vbar (velocity vector). The Orbiter then slowly inched toward the docking port at the forward end of the U.S.-built Destiny laboratory module, the docking port always used by the Space Shuttle.

After the docking was completed, the photos were downlinked through the station's Ku-band communications system for analysis by systems engineers and mission managers.

Discovery's crew cabin and the Orbiter Docking System (ODS) as imaged during the mapping sequence photographed by the Expedition 11 crew during the Rbar Pitch Maneuver on Flight Day 3. This image was taken with the 800mm lens. (NASA)

The Forward Reaction Control System (FRCS) module on Discovery, *taken with the 800mm lens. The light grey nose cap is made of Reinforced Carbon-Carbon, similar to the wing leading edges. The FRCS itself is covered with a series of tiles and blankets.* (NASA)

A slightly wider-angle view of the crew compartment and ODS taken with the 400mm lens. The Ku-Band antenna just forward of the right payload bay door is used for high-bandwidth communications and also as a radar during docking operations. Note that the Ku radar is still tracking the ISS during the early part of the RPM since it's pointing directly toward the photographer. (NASA)

Good details of the windscreen area taken with the 400mm lens. The Ku-Band antenna is at the right. Note the unusual pattern of black tiles under the pilot's (right) windscreen; these were part of the original tile pattern based on early predictions of heating. Later measurements have shown the black tiles are unnecessary in this location and they are replaced by white tiles when needed. (NASA)

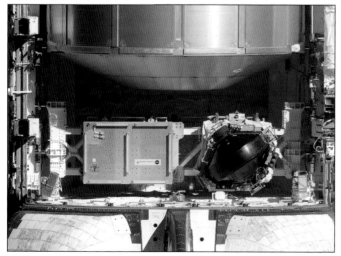

A Control Moment Gyroscope (CMG) and the Thermal Protection System Repair (DTO-848) test article were stowed along the aft bulkhead of the payload bay. The ISS uses CMGs for attitude control and Discovery was delivering a replacement unit. DTO-848 tested tile repair techniques during an EVA. The 400mm lens was used. (NASA)

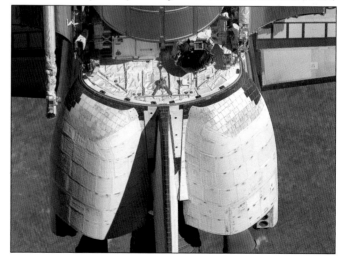

The Orbital Maneuvering System (OMS) pods, taken with the 400mm lens. The small circles along each side of the vertical stabilizer are exhaust ports for the Auxiliary Power Units (APU #1 and #2 on the left; APU #3 at the rear on the right) and Water Spray Boilers (the others on the right). (NASA)

John Phillips used the 400mm lens for this photo of Discovery during the Rbar Pitch Maneuver, and it quickly became a favorite of many magazines and newspapers. The Ku-Band antenna, still tracking the ISS, is at the right while the Shuttle Remote Manipulator System arm is at the left. The white circles show the gap fillers that came loose and worried engineers enough to have the astronauts remove them prior to entry (see page 63). (NASA)

The elevons on the right wing taken with the 400mm lens. Each elevon is supported by three hinges and the gap between the elevon and the wing is covered by a series of "flipper doors" that show up as a series of black-and-white squares. (NASA)

The business end of the Orbiter shows three Space Shuttle Main engines (SSMEs, the large nozzles), two Orbital Maneuvering System (OMS) engines (the intermediate-size nozzles on the OMS pods), and four Reaction Control System (RCS) thrusters (the two small nozzles next to each OMS engine). The body flap under the main engines provides pitch control trim during atmospheric flight but has no function while on-orbit. (NASA)

A slightly different view of the SSMEs and base heat shield taken with the 400mm lens. Note the areas around the SSMEs that allow the engines to gimbal for directional control during ascent. (NASA)

800mm views of the Orbiter windscreens. The two star tracker openings are on the right. The black tiles around the center windows are needed because of entry heating, but the odd black tiles under the pilot's window will be replaced by white tiles if the need arises. Note Andy Thomas in the pilot's seat. (NASA)

This photo caused some alarm because the thermal blanket under the commander's side window is not supposed to be "puffed out" (see page 55). The markings (such as the Discovery name) are created with Dow-Corning 3140 silicon-based paint. (NASA)

The bottom of the nose taken with the 800mm lens. The forward landing gear doors show up well, as does the intricate pattern of the Thermal Protection System tiles. The nose cap, chin panel (between the nose cap and the front of the landing gear doors) and the ET attach point (a triangle just behind the doors) are made from Reinforced Carbon-Carbon. (NASA)

The bottom of the body flap as seen through the 800mm lens. The discoloration of the tiles just ahead of the body flap is due to oxidation and heat during entry. In general, the very black tiles are new replacements, while older tiles gradually turn light grey with brownish streaks. The gaps between the elevons and the fuselage are large by aircraft standards. (NASA)

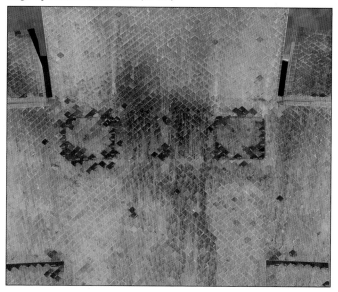

Taken with the 400mm lens. Note the Ku-band radar is no longer tracking the ISS – it lost track during the RPM when the wing and payload bay door blocked the line-of-sight. (NASA)

The two squares with new (blacker) tiles around the edges are the doors over the External Tank umbilicals. These doors are open during ascent when the ET is connected. (NASA)

Return to Flight – Space Shuttle Discovery

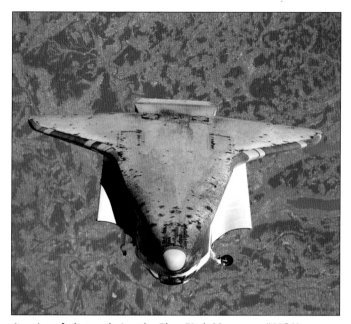

A series of photos during the Rbar Pitch Maneuver. (NASA)

VISITING THE ISS

The major objectives of STS-114, besides the "test flight" aspect of checking the post-Columbia hardware fixes, was to deliver cargo to the International Space Station. Mission specialist Wendy Lawrence was in charge of transferring cargo from the *Raffaello* MPLM to the ISS.

A small (but heavy) piece of cargo in the back of the payload bay was also important. Four Control Moment Gyros (CMG) on the Z1 truss provide attitude control for the ISS without needing to burn propellants like the thrusters on the Russian segment. One of these CMGs had failed in June 2002.

The failed gyro was replaced during the second EVA using the Canadarm 2 on the ISS to move the CMGs back and forth to *Discovery*'s payload bay.

Each CMG weighs 620 pounds, is about the size of a washing machine, and has a reaction wheel that spins at a constant speed of 6,600 revolutions per minute. Repositioning gyros' spin axes causes the CMGs to generate torque that is transferred to the station structure. This counteracts gravitational and drag forces to maintain attitude or induce changes to the station's orientation.

Discovery transitioning between the Rbar and Vbar for the final approach to the ISS. Note the aft end of the Soyuz spacecraft in the foreground. This photo was taken from the Pirs docking compartment. The Orbiter docked at 07:18 EDT on Thursday, 28 July 2005. (NASA)

A full payload bay. Along the rear bulkhead are the Control Moment Gyro and Thermal Protection System Repair DTO-848 test article. The Raffaello Multi-Purpose Logistics Module takes up most of the rear half of the bay. The External Stowage Platform 2 (ESP-2) is just forward of Raffaello and the Orbiter Docking System is at the extreme front. ESP-2 carries Orbital Replacement Units for the ISS. (NASA)

The Ku-Band antenna is carried on the starboard side of the forward payload bay. (NASA)

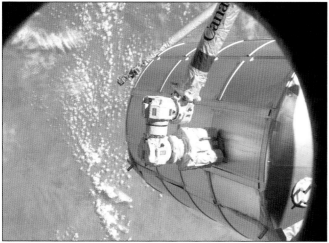

Soyuz TMA-6 spacecraft docked to the Zarya functional cargo block on the ISS. Note the periscope protruding from Soyuz on the top (in the photo) side. Since the Columbia accident, Soyuz has been the only method for astronauts to reach the ISS, and one is always docked at the station to allow the crew to return in the event of an emergency. The Shuttle Remote Manipulator System (RMS) arm and the Space Station Remote Manipulator System (SSRMS) Canadarm 2 are partially visible in the background. (NASA)

Canadarm 2 moves Raffaello from Discovery's payload bay to its temporary berth on the station's Unity node. Once berthed at the ISS, crewmembers unloaded supplies from the MPLM and loaded it with material and trash for the return to Earth. (NASA)

Eileen Collins goes over a checklist dealing with rendezvous and docking operations while seated at the commander's station onboard Discovery. (NASA)

Collins prepares to open the hatch that will allow access to the ISS. Note the gauge just below her arm indicates zero differential pressure. (NASA)

John Phillips, Eileen Collins, Soichi Noguchi, Charlie Camarda, and Steve Robinson take a break in the Zvezda service module of the station. (NASA)

Not since 2002 had nine crewmembers been on the International Space Station. Eileen Collins waves from upper right. Clockwise from her are Charlie Camarda, Soichi Noguchi, Wendy Lawrence, Sergei Krikalev, James Kelly, Andy Thomas, and John Phillips. Steve Robinson took the photo with a digital still camera in the Destiny laboratory module. Note the flags on the rear bulkhead. (NASA)

Steve Robinson, holding a video camera, floats in the hatch leading to the Zvezda service module. There are hand-holds located all over the interior of the ISS to assist crewmembers moving around in the microgravity environment. (NASA)

Steve Robinson floats in the Destiny laboratory module holding a video camera. The light blue stripes on his pants are velcro strips to attach things to so they do not drift off. There are signs saying "deck" and "overhead" around most hatches. (NASA)

Expedition 11 flight engineer and science officer John Phillips holds a microphone as he rings the ship's bell in the Destiny laboratory module. Note that Phillips name tag is in both English and Cyrillic in deference to Russia's large participation in the ISS. (NASA)

Charlie Camarda smiles for the camera as he talks to the ground from communications equipment in the Unity node. A Nikon camera floats in front of him. Note the sign pointing to the Zarya FGB module. (NASA)

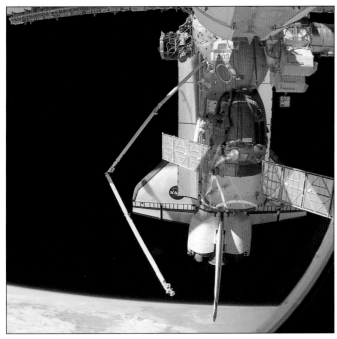

A view of Discovery taken from the Pirs docking compartment. Visible in the frame are the the Shuttle Remote Manipulator System (RMS) arm with the Orbiter Boom Sensor System (OBSS) attached and the Soyuz vehicle docked with the ISS. (NASA)

Cosmonaut Sergei Krikalev (left) and astronaut John Phillips pose for a photo in the Zvezda service module. (NASA)

Wide-angle view, taken from Destiny's optical-quality window, of Discovery with the Raffaello MPLM at the top of the frame. (NASA)

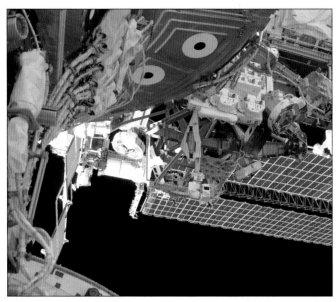

The Canadian-built Mobile Base System (MBS) is an aluminum work platform designed to move along the space station's side rails. The Canadarm2 attaches to the MBS. (NASA)

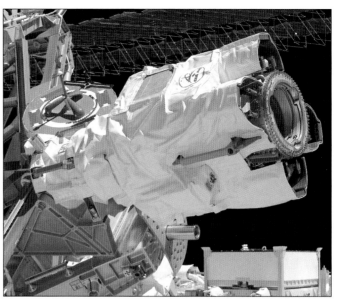

This is the Payload ORU Accommodation (POA) on the Mobile Base System installed on the Port One (P1) truss of the International Space Station. (NASA)

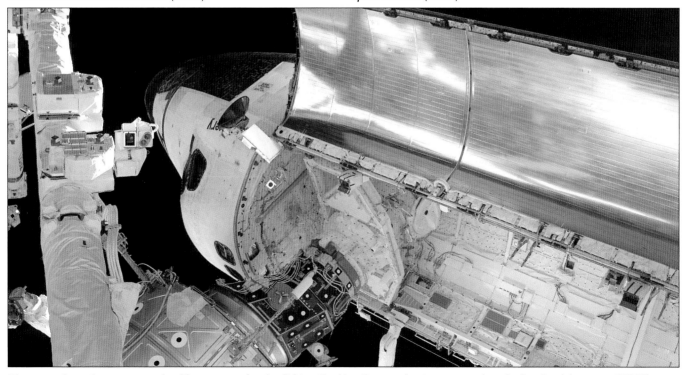

Discovery shows her empty payload bay, except for the Orbiter Docking System that is connected to the Destiny laboratory. (NASA)

The Expedition 11 and STS-114 crewmembers gather for a group photo in the Destiny laboratory module. In the front row (from left) are Andy Thomas, Eileen Collins, Sergei Krikalev, and John Phillips. In the back row (from left) are Soichi Noguchi, James Kelly, Charlie Camarda, Wendy Lawrence, and Steve Robinson. Land's End does good business supplying shirts. (NASA)

Wendy Lawrence looks over a procedures checklist in the Destiny laboratory module. Sergei Krikalev, Expedition 11 is in the background. The pair is in the process of transferring material from the Orbiter to the ISS. (NASA)

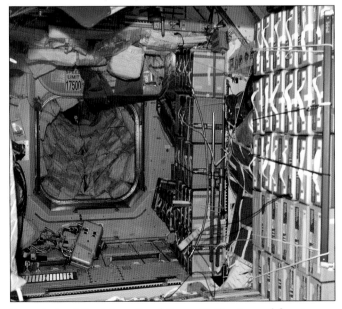

Every inch of the International Space Station is used for storage. Here, stowage bags are packed into the Pressurized Mating Adapter 1 (PMA1) and food canisters line the wall in the Unity node. (NASA)

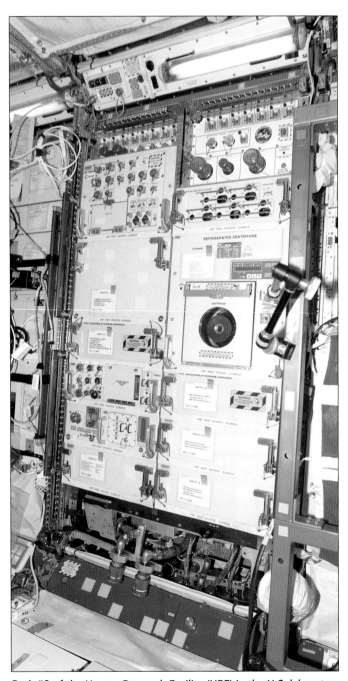

Rack #2 of the Human Research Facility (HRF) in the U.S. laboratory of the ISS. The HRF provides an on-orbit laboratory to study the physiological, behavioral, and chemical changes in human beings induced by space flight. (NASA)

A blanket directly under the Commander's side window was found to be "puffed out" and torn. This condition had never been seen on-orbit before, and there was no obvious explanation for how the blanket was damaged. In the end, no action was taken. (NASA)

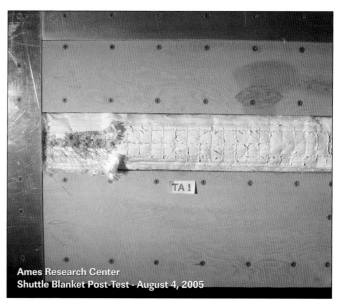

After the cockpit blanket anomaly was discovered, the NASA Ames Research Center used its wind tunnels to determine that the blanket would likely not be further damaged during entry. This was the test setup in one of the Ames wind tunnels. (NASA)

Stowage bags packed in the Raffaello Multi-Purpose Logistics Module (MPLM) while it was docked to the ISS. Each of the 21-foot-long, 15-foot-diameter MLPMs can carry up to 10 tons of cargo packed into 16 standard space station equipment racks. (NASA)

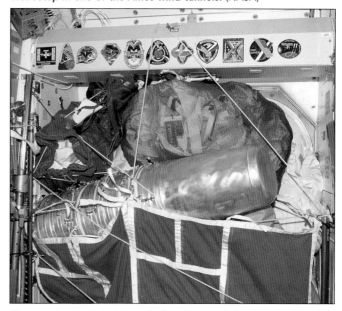

Stowage bags packed into the hatch area of the Unity node. Note the eleven ISS Expedition patches on the bulkhead. Expedition 11 was resident on the ISS while STS-114 was docked, and Expedition 12 replaced them in October 2005. (NASA)

SPACEWALKS

Three extravehicular activities (EVA) were planned on STS-114, and all were completed successfully. Soichi Noguchi and Steve Robinson were the designated spacewalkers for the mission. The EVAs began and ended in the Orbiter airlock, although the outer hatch of the Quest airlock remained open during all three EVAs in case somebody needed to get back inside quickly during an emergency.

The first EVA took place on Flight Day 5, and was dedicated primarily to testing repair techniques for the Orbiter Thermal Protection System. These tests were part of Detailed Test Objective (DTO) 848 and included evaluations of the emittance wash (EW) applicator and the NOAX (non-oxide adhesive, experimental) RCC crack repair technique. Both experiments were conducted on special samples carried up in the payload bay, and not on real Orbiter surfaces.

The second EVA was on Flight Day 7 and was dedicated to replacing the Control Moment Gyro on the ISS.

The third EVA was on Flight Day 9, and was originally intended for a variety of tasks such as mounting a new camera on the ISS and the installation and retrieval of several experiments from the outside of the station. However, after analysts noticed two gap fillers protruding from between tiles on the underside of the Orbiter, NASA's attention turned to removing them. The gap fillers – used to keep the fragile tiles from rubbing against each other as the expand and contract from heating – had slipped out of position and protruded up to 1.1-inches from the bottom of the Orbiter. Engineers worried these might "trip" the boundary layer and cause unacceptable heating levels during entry. Robinson successfully removed both of them during the third EVA using his gloved hand.

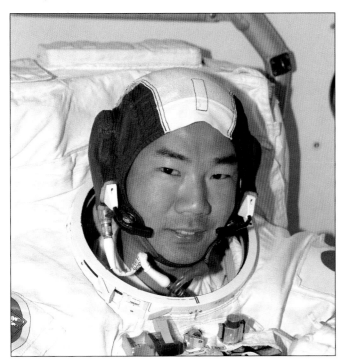 

Soichi Noguchi (left) and Steve Robinson in their Extravehicular Mobility Units (EMU) – minus the helmets – in Discovery's airlock. (NASA)

Soichi Noguchi traverses along the Destiny laboratory; the photograph was taken by Steve Robinson. Noguchi was designated EV1, and wore a spacesuit marked by red stripes on the legs. Robinson was EV2 and wore a spacesuit that was all white. In the left hand photo, Noguchi is next to the optical quality window on the Destiny lab. The window is covered with a protective shutter when not in use. (NASA)

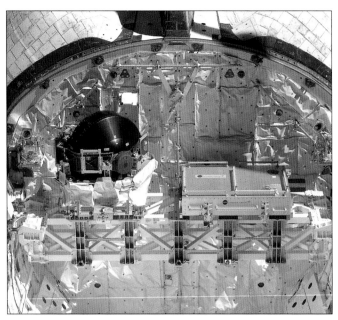

Excellent view of the control moment gyro (CMG) and DTO-848 Thermal Protection System repair test equipment secured to the aft bulkhead of the payload bay. (NASA)

Steve Robinson in the Orbiter mid-deck holding some of the tools he will use during the second extravehicular activity (EVA) of the mission. Note the humorous tee-shirt. (NASA)

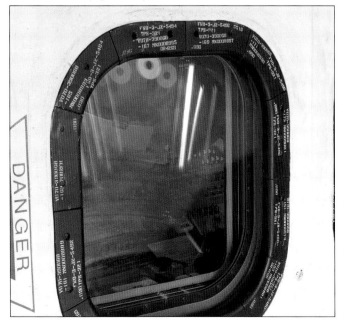

Details of the upper-left flight deck window, as seen during the first EVA. This window can be explosively jettisoned (note red warning next to it) to allow the astronauts to escape on the ground. (NASA)

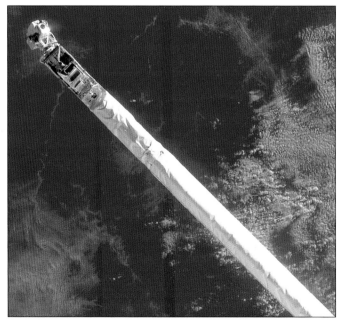

The sensor package on the end of the Orbiter Boom Sensor System (OBSS) that was flown for the first time on STS-114. This package was used to survey the Orbiter for damage. (NASA)

Fish-eye view of the aft end of the empty payload bay taken during preparations for the first extravehicular activity (EVA) of the mission. Visible in the frame are the Control Moment Gyro and the Thermal Protection System Repair DTO-848 in their berthed positions along the aft bulkhead. The External Stowage Platform 2 is visible in the foreground. Radiators line each payload bay door. (NASA)

It is a tight squeeze in the Orbiter's airlock. Steve Robinson (left) and Soichi Noguchi prepare for the first of three EVAs in their *Extravehicular Mobility Units.* (NASA)

This is the view of the blue Earth behind Discovery as Robinson and Noguchi exited the airlock. Portions of the wing, payload bay sill, and OMS pod are visible. (NASA)

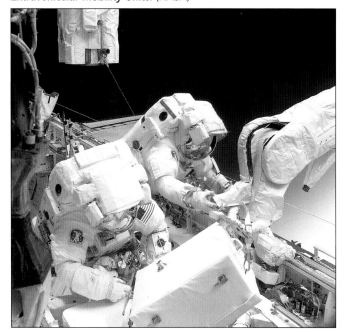

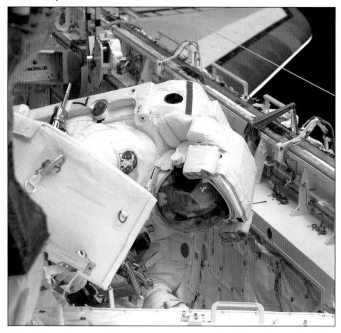

Steve Robinson (left) and Soichi Noguchi unpack equipment and attach it to Canadarm 2 while in Discovery's payload bay during the first EVA. Note the cuff checklists attached the left sleeve of their EMU and the national flag patches on the shoulder. (NASA)

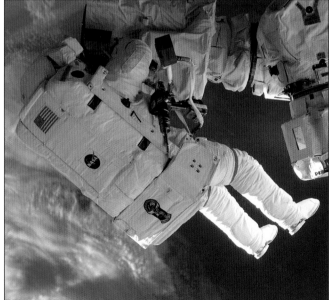

Soichi Noguchi climbs aboard the Space Station Remote Manipulator System (SSRMS) Canadarm 2 during the first extravehicular activity. Noguchi and Steve Robinson (not shown) demonstrated Orbiter Thermal Protection System repair techniques, and completed enhancements to the International Space Station's attitude control system during the 6-hour, 50-minute spacewalk (NASA)

Soichi Noguchi at work inside the P1 truss. The "T" structure at the top is a UHF antenna. Just to its right is a WETA (wireless external transceiver assembly) used for wireless video. Also visible along the top and bottom of the truss are the trunnion pins that were used to secure the truss segment in the payload bay of Endeavour that carried P1 to the ISS as part of STS-113 in November 2002. (NASA)

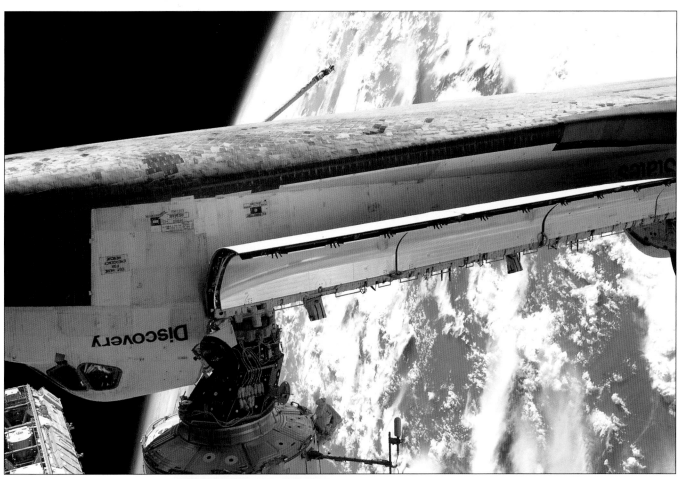

Discovery *docked to PMA2 on the Destiny laboratory module. The "T" structure on the side of Destiny is another UHF antenna. In the lower left, the ISS truss structure is visible.* (NASA)

Soichi Noguchi works his way down the S0 truss. Equipment is located everywhere aboard the station, as evidenced here. A U.S. solar array from the P6 truss segment is visible in the background. (NASA)

Noguchi signals okay to the camera during the first extravehicular activity. His hand and part of the payload bay are reflected in his helmet visor. (NASA)

The three STS-114 EVAs originated in Discovery's airlock and were the 26th, 27th, and 28th Shuttle-based EVAs out of 61 spacewalks that have been conducted to assemble the space station. (NASA)

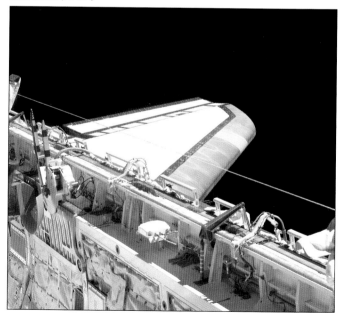

The port sill of the Orbiter payload bay. The line running above the sill is an EVA slidewire. At the far left is one of the Manipulator Positioning Mechanisms (MPM) used to stow the RMS. (NASA)

A great view of Discovery during one of the STS-114 EVAs. The Space Station Remote Manipulator System (SSRMS) Canadarm 2 is partially visible extended beside the Orbiter. The two "holes" just ahead of the windscreens are the star trackers that provide navigational data to the Orbiter on-orbit. The crew hatch used on the ground is at the top center. (NASA)

Note that in addition to the foot restraints, Steve is secured using two safety tethers. Mounted to the back of the EMU is SAFER (Simplified Aid For EVA Rescue), a jetpack that uses cold-gas nitrogen to propel the astronaut back to safety should both tethers become unfastened. These precautions are necessary because it is unlikely that a Soyuz or the Orbiter could undock quickly enough to rescue a stranded EVA crewmember. (NASA)

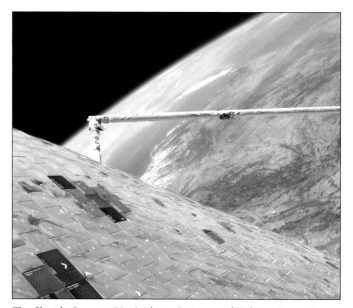

Large radiators are located inside the payload bay doors. Each door can support two two-panel radiators (as shown here). The total heat rejection capacity of the radiators is 30,550 BTUs. Each of the four panels per side is 15.1 feet long and 10.5 feet wide. (NASA)

The Shuttle Remote Manipulator System and Orbiter Boom Sensor System arms as seen during one of the EVAs. The OBSS instrument package consists of the Laser Camera System (LCS) and a Laser Dynamic Range Imager (LDRI). (NASA)

STS-114 was the first time that astronauts had ventured underneath the Orbiter while on-orbit. It also represented the most detailed tile survey taken on-orbit, checking for damage that could be catastrophic during entry. The black High-temperature Reusable Surface Insulation (HRSI) tiles are used on areas of the Orbiter that are subjected to temperatures between 1,200 and 2,300 degrees Fahrenheit. Areas where the temperature exceeds 2,300 degrees use Reinforced Carbon-Carbon. (NASA)

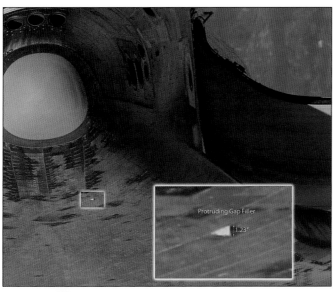

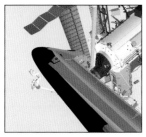

During a review of images from the Rbar Pitch Maneuver, analysts found two gap fillers protruding from between tiles in the Thermal Protection System near the nose landing gear doors. One of the gap fillers protruded about 1.1 inches, while the other protruded 0.6 inch. Both gap fillers were the Ames type, which is a thin layer (~0.020-inch) of Nextel fabric coated with a light gray ceramic material. It is fairly flexible with a brittle coating. These gap fillers are bonded to the filler bar (pad bonded to Orbiter surface between tile gaps) with red RTV adhesive. Engineers worried the protruding gap fillers could "trip" the hypersonic boundary layer, creating extremely high turbulent heating downstream during entry. Computer simulations were non-conclusive in eliminating this concern, so NASA decided to remove the two gap fillers during an EVA. Steve Robinson used the Canadarm 2 to position himself below the Orbiter, and easily removed the gap fillers using his gloved hand (TV images at right). If that had not worked, Robinson would have tried forceps (shown being practiced on the ground at left), or as a last result, a hack saw (below left and center) to cut the gap fillers off flush with the tile. The repair took 66 minutes and the gap fillers are now in the National Air and Space Museum. (NASA)

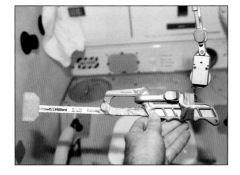

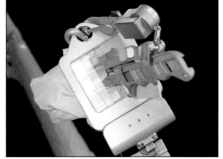

The chine area, wing leading edge, and payload doors of Discovery. Note the repairs (darker, wavy lines) to the Nomex felt reusable surface insulation (FRSI) blankets and Steve Robinson's shadow on the payload bay doors. (NASA)

View of the space station's S1 truss during the third EVA. The two Crew Equipment Translation Assembly (CETA) carts in Bay 7 are visible in their stowed position, and the Canadarm 2 is visible. A small portion of the Orbiter is shown in the upper right. (NASA)

Steve Robinson aims the camera at himself, with the underside of Discovery in the background. Robinson and Noguchi spent a total of 20 hours and 5 minutes outside the vehicle during the three EVAs performed during STS-114. (NASA)

A dramatic shot of the underside of the nose. Note the complex pattern of the tiles, designed to assist high-speed airflow during entry. The nose landing gear doors are clearly visible, and small damaged areas can be seen along the rear edge. (NASA)

The different colors of the tiles are indicative of when they were installed on the vehicle. Despite common misperceptions, very few tiles are replaced after each mission, and a majority of the tiles on OV-103 have been there since the Orbiter was delivered in 1983. The ones that are replaced are frequently over antennas. Here, the darker tiles cover (top row, left to right) the radar altimeter 1 transmitter, TACAN 3 lower/S-Band FM lower hemi, radar altimeter 2 receiver, S-Band PM lower right quad, (second row): UHF antenna, (third row) Radar altimeter 2 transmitter, (bottom) TACAN 2 lower. (NASA)

While perched in Bay 08 of the S0 truss, Soichi Noguchi acts as observer and communication relay station between fellow spacewalker Steve Robinson (out of frame) and Andy Thomas aboard the Orbiter during the third EVA. (NASA)

As Discovery floats over a desert, the astronauts continued snapping photos of the underside of the Orbiter. Steve Robinson remarked, "Maybe you have to be an old aerodynamicist like me, but the surface of this belly is just a work of art." (NASA)

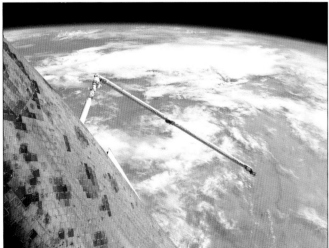

Another great view of the complex tile pattern around the nose landing gear doors. Just ahead of the doors is the Reinforced Carbon-Carbon chin panel. This panel was installed because the black tiles were originally located there on Columbia were constantly damaged during landing by debris kicked up off the lake beds at Edwards Air Force Base. Part of the S0 truss is visible in front of the P6 truss in the background. (NASA)

The entire 50-foot length of the Orbiter Boom Sensor System arm. The OBSS was implemented quickly when it was believed that Space Shuttles would return to flight in late 2003 or early 2004. The boom consists of two graphite-epoxy cylinders originally manufactured as spares for the Remote Manipulator System (RMS) arms. (NASA)

Note the caution markings on the side of Discovery advising rescue crews how to get into the Orbiter in the event it should crash during landing. This is typical military practice, and the markings are universally understood by crash teams worldwide. The forward portion of the chines are covered by black tiles, while most of the wing leading edge is composed of RCC panels. (NASA)

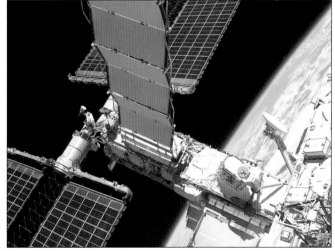

One of the P6 truss Solar Array Wings (SAW), Mast Canisters, Photovoltaic (PV) Radiator, and Solar Array Blanket Boxes (SABB) on the International Space Station. The ISS is totally dependent on solar arrays to provide normal power. The large ISS Ku-band communications antenna is at the right edge of the photo. (NASA)

There are two windows (one shown here) on the aft flight deck of the Orbiter that look into the payload bay. The windows are fairly small, only 14.5 x 11-inches. Note the dark-colored pins around the upper edge of the fuselage where the payload bay doors latch when they are closed. (NASA)

The Orbiters dock to the Destiny laboratory at the ISS, unlike Soyuz and Progress that dock to the Russian modules. Part of the P1 and S0 trusses and a solar array are visible in the background. (NASA)

Steve Robinson having some fun photographing his shadow against the bottom of Discovery. Robinson was standing on a platform at the end of the ISS's Canadarm 2. (NASA)

The primary payload for STS-114 was the Italian-built Raffaello Multi-Purpose Logistics Module. The MPLM is a pressurized cargo container used to transport racks, equipment, and supplies to the ISS. The MPLM is removed from the payload bay using the Canadarm 2 (foreground) and connected to the ISS using the Common Berthing Mechanism, which locks it in place with an airtight seal on the nadir side of the Unity node. The MPLM carried about 4,000 pounds of cargo, including a medical experiment rack, to the ISS, and approximately 5,000 pounds of material and trash was returned to Earth. A small part of a Soyuz solar array may be seen behind the MPLM. (NASA)

Steve Robinson anchored to a foot restraint on the Canadarm 2 during the third EVA. (NASA)

Return to Flight – Space Shuttle Discovery

GOING HOME

After the third EVA, the crews began to prepare for *Discovery* to depart the ISS and head home. The *Raffaello* MPLM was loaded with material and trash that needed to be returned to Earth, sealed, undocked from the ISS, and stowed back in the payload bay of the Orbiter.

When *Discovery* was ready to undock, Charlie Camarda sent a command to release the docking mechanism. During initial separation of the spacecraft, springs in the docking mechanism pushed the Orbiter away from the Destiny laboratory. *Discovery*'s Reaction Control System thrusters were inhibited during the initial separation. *Discovery* was pushed away from the ISS at 3:24 a.m. (EDT) on 6 August 2005.

Once *Discovery* was about two feet from the Station, with the docking devices clear of one another, James Kelly enabled the RCS thrusters on and fired them to slowly move away. From the aft flight deck, Kelly manually controlled *Discovery* within a tight corridor as the Orbiter separated from the station, essentially the reverse of the task performed by Eileen Collins just before *Discovery* docked.

Discovery continued away to a distance of about 450 feet, where Vegas initiated a maneuver to fly the Orbiter directly above the ISS. Since the Orbiter had sufficient propellants remaining, it did a flyaround the ISS to permit *Discovery*'s crew to photograph the station; these photos would be analyzed for damage or other areas of concern once *Discovery* was safely on the ground. Once the flyaround was completed, Kelly used the RCS to depart the vicinity of the ISS and set up a standard orbit while the crew prepared to head home.

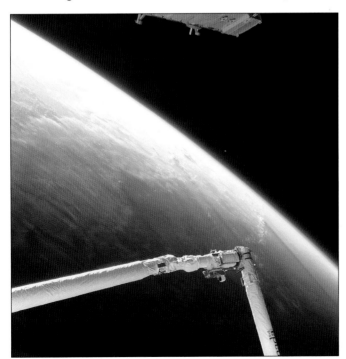 

The blackness of space and Earth's horizon form the backdrop for the Remote Manipulator System and Orbiter Boom Sensor System as seen by the STS-114 crew while docked to the International Space Station. It was almost time for Discovery to return to Earth. (NASA)

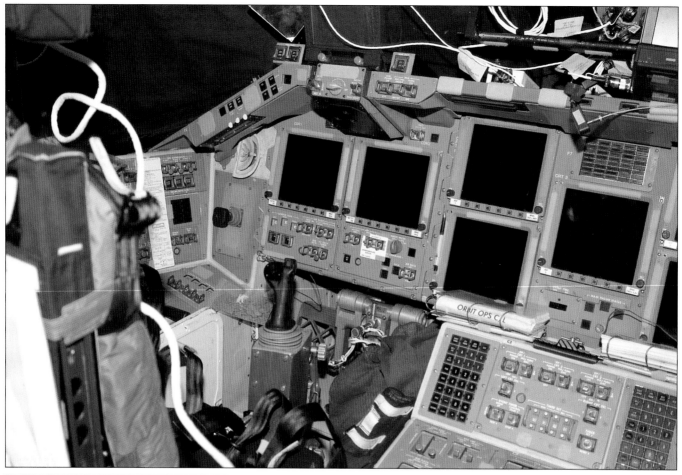

The instrument panel at the commander's station on the flight deck of Discovery. All of the Orbiters have now been updated with "glass cockpits," called the Multifunction Electronic Display System (MEDS) by NASA. There are two displays in front of each pilot, five in the center of the main instrument panel, and two at the aft station. Each display is 6.71-inches square. (NASA)

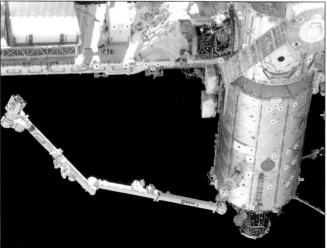

In this photo, the Space Station Remote Manipulator System is mounted on the Destiny laboratory module. Canadarm 2 is a larger, more advanced version of the Canadarm used as the space Shuttle Remote Manipulator System arm. Canadarm 2 was installed on the International Space Station in April 2001, with the help of Canadian astronaut Chris Hadfield. Canadarm 2 is 55 feet long and has seven motorized joints. (NASA)

The instrument panel at the pilot's station on the flight deck of Discovery. The astronauts input data to the system through edgekeys around the periphery of the panels and through the keyboards on the center console. Both pilots also have heads-up displays (HUD) and a rotational hand controller. The center panels are still labeled "CRT" even though the technology is actually LCD. (NASA)

Discovery with the Earth in the background photographed by the Expedition 11 crew after undocking. The Raffaello MPLM is in the rear of the payload bay, but the External Stowage Platform-2 was left on the ISS. The Orbiter Boom Sensor System has been reberthed on the starboard payload bay sill and the Shuttle Remote Manipulator System is above the port sill. The Ku-band antenna is tracking the ISS. (NASA)

Sergei Krikalev (left) and Eileen Collins pose in the Unity node after the STS-114 crew patch was added to the growing collection of insignias on the International Space Station. (NASA)

The port wing of the Orbiter. The lighter grey panels on the wing leading edge are new Reinforced Carbon-Carbon panels, while the darker ones are older and more oxidized. (NASA)

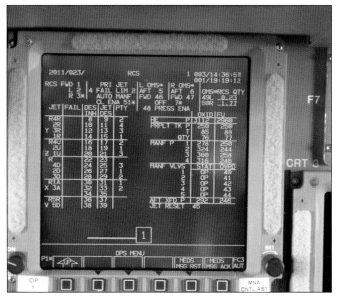

Although the new Multifunction Electronic Display System (MEDS) hardware is capable of full-color operation, many of the displays emulate the old green phosphor used by the original CRTs. This particular display provides status and control over the Reaction Control System (RCS) jets and propellant manifolds. (NASA)

James Kelly holding a procedures checklist while on the aft flight deck. The inside of the Orbiter is decidedly less organized while on-orbit than while on the ground, with a myriad of cables and equipment spread around every available space. The pilot's position on the flight deck is to the left of the photo. (NASA)

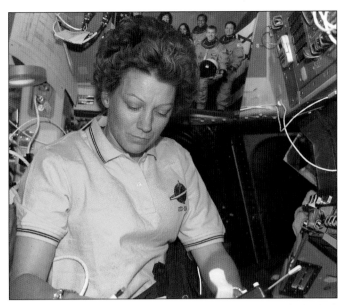

Eileen Collins works at her station on Discovery's forward flight deck during undocking with the ISS. The STS-107 (Columbia) crew portrait crew is visible on the bulkhead behind her head, a constant reminder of the dangers of space flight. (NASA)

Eileen Collins (left) and James Kelly begin setting up Discovery to come home. Although the MEDS system replaced the old CRTs with new LCD displays, the original keyboards (being used by Collins) were retained. (NASA)

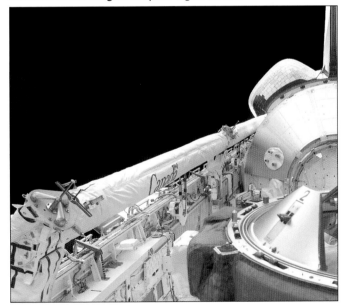

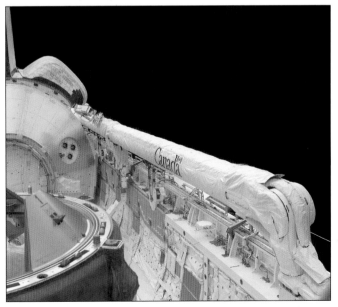

A view of the payload bay from the aft windows. The Orbiter Docking System is in the foreground and the Raffaello Multi-Purpose Logistics Module is in the background. The Shuttle Remote Manipulator System arm is berthed on the port sill and the Orbiter Boom Sensor System is berthed on the starboard sill. The RMS has an articulated joint where it attaches to the sill (lower right corner), while the OBSS is not permanently attached to the Orbiter, being attached to the RMS during use. (NASA)

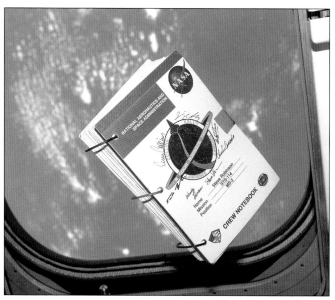

"Stevie Ray" Robinson's crew notebook (covered with his crews' signatures) floating in front of the upper flight deck window. If this book ever found its way to eBay, it would sell for a fortune, being a signed – and flown – item. (NASA)

Not everything is built into the Orbiter. Here an IBM ThinkPad 760XD runs the World Map application that displays the Orbiter's position over the Earth. Showing the march of technology, the laptop is more powerful than all five of the Orbiter's computers combined. (NASA)

The Mach 25 patch is awarded only to astronauts who have flown on the Space Shuttle, the only winged vehicle capable of reaching 25 times the speed of sound. Astronaut Rick Hauck designed the patch. Eileen Collins presents patches to STS-114's two rookie astronauts – Charlie Camarda (left) and Soichi Noguchi. Reportedly, the first evidence of the patch is a 1984 photo where it can be seen on the blue flight suit of Robert Crippen. It is assumed that the patch was first given to the crew of STS-7, which was the first flight for Rick Hauck. (NASA)

ISS FLYAROUND

The first Space Shuttle flyaround of a space station was during the Shuttle-Mir program, on STS-63 in 1995 when *Discovery* performed a close approach of *Mir* but did not dock. The primary purpose of a flyaround is for photography. While public relations has always been a strong motivator for getting photographs, they have also proven extremely useful as "closeout" photos showing the actual state of the station after an assembly flight, and for planning future EVAs. After the Progress-Mir collision in 1997, subsequent flyaround photography attempted to pinpoint the location of the leak in the Spektr module.

Flyarounds are usually rather low in the list of mission priorities, and are always contingent on having enough propellant available. With competing demands on Orbiter propellant, such as ISS reboost, the flyaround is sometimes truncated or deleted.

Starting with STS-71, the first Shuttle-Mir docking mission, flyarounds have traditionally been flown by the Orbiter pilot (PLT). This provides valuable real-world experience in proximity operations for pilots before they fly their first approach and docking as a mission commander (CDR).

Ironically, Eileen Collins never got the benefit of that experience prior to STS-114. On her first flight, STS-63, the flyaround was performed by the CDR, James Wetherbee. On her second flight, STS-84, the flyaround was replaced by a straight-line separation down the Rbar to test a European rendezvous sensor that was a candidate for the ESA Automated Transfer Vehicle (ATV). Her third flight, STS-93, was a non-station mission. James Kelly, on the other hand, had flown an ISS flyaround on his first flight, STS-102 in 2001.

Forward view showing the Pressurized Mating Adapter 2, the Destiny laboratory module, the Space Station Remote Manipulator System, the Quest airlock, a Soyuz spacecraft docked to Zarya, and the External Stowage Platform 2 attached to the Quest airlock. (NASA)

Backdropped by the blackness of space, this nadir view of the International Space Station shows the Unity node, the Quest airlock, and the Destiny laboratory module. All of these modules were supplied by the United States. (NASA)

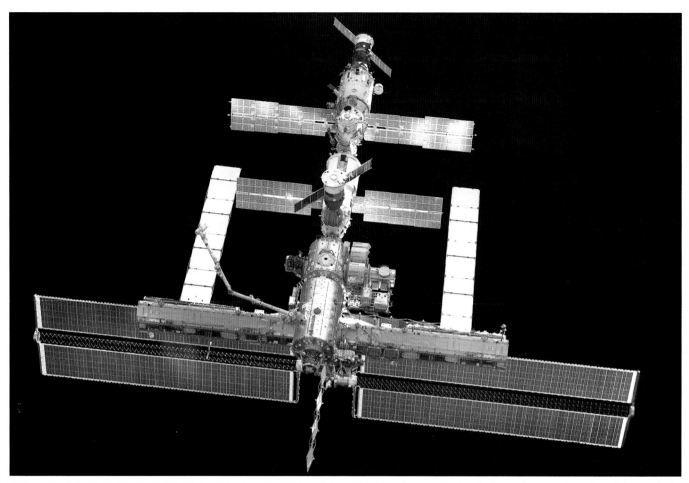

This view from nadir clearly shows the main line of modules, with the US Destiny laboratory module (forward) at the bottom of the photo and the Russian segment (aft) at top. Running from left to right along the bottom of the photo is the partially completed main truss mounted to Destiny. Behind that is the P6 truss segment and its two large solar array wings. Future ISS assembly flights will attach more truss segments with three more pairs of solar arrays, and relocate P6 to the end of the truss for a total of four pairs. (NASA)

Aft view of ISS. In the foreground are the Zarya FGB module, the Zvezda service module, and the Progress spacecraft. The US segment is in the background. (NASA)

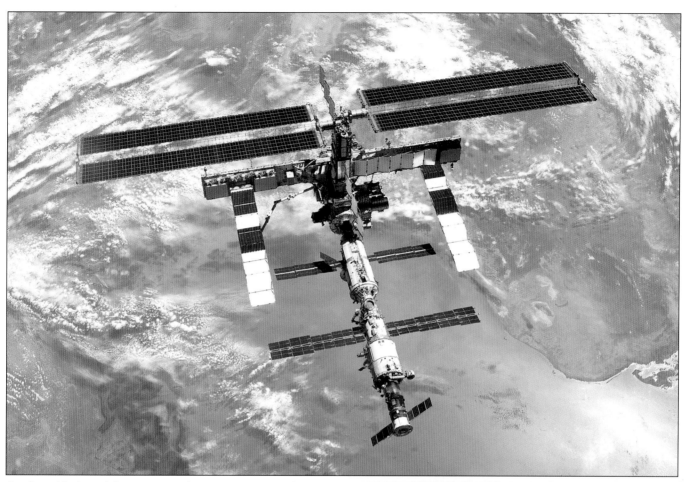

An aft zenith view of the International Space Station over the North Caspian Sea and Kazakhstan. In this view, the velocity vector is toward the top of the photo. After the Orbiter begins the flyaround, the ISS maneuvers to a torque equilibrium attitude (TEA) that attempts to balance the torques on the vehicle to minimize propellant required for attitude control. This results in a visible yaw to the left to balance the extra drag caused by Quest and the large radiator on the starboard side. Notice the large radiators extending aft from the main truss; there are two more radiators on each side that are not yet deployed. When they are, the Zarya solar arrays will need to be retracted so as not to interfere with the radiators. (NASA)

Visible in this photo are the Unity node and the Soyuz spacecraft docked to the Zarya module. (NASA)

Nadir view of the International Space Station. (NASA)

A forward zenith view of ISS showing the Destiny laboratory, S0, S1, P1, and P6 trusses, Pressurized Mating Adapter 2, Zvezda service module, Zarya FGB module, Progress logistics spacecraft, and the Space Station Remote Manipulator System. (NASA)

Aft zenith view showing the Russian Progress logistics spacecraft docked to the Zvezda service module. While the Space Shuttle fleet was grounded in 2003–2006, the Progress was the primary supply vehicle for the ISS. (NASA)

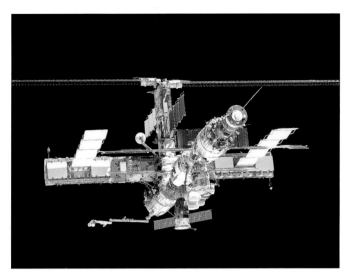

Aft nadir view of the International Space Station. (NASA)

Aft zenith view showing the Zarya FGB module and the Zvezda service module. Note the unoccupied zenith docking port on Zvezda. Originally, this port was to be occupied by the Russian science power platform (SPP). As part of a US–Russian barter deal, the SPP was to be carried to ISS by two Space Shuttle flights. As of this writing, the SPP is a candidate for deletion in order to minimize the number of Space Shuttle flights required to complete ISS. To compensate for the loss of electrical power, more power would be transferred from the American segment to the Russian segment. (NASA)

Aft zenith view of the ISS over the North Caspian Sea with the Volga River entering from the bottom of the image. This view is actually looking to the southeast from the bottom of the frame across the Caspian at the top of the frame. (NASA)

THE ALTERNATIVES

While the Space Shuttle was grounded, the International Space Station was completely dependent upon the Russian Space Agency to provide supplies and crew rotation. Fortunately, the Russians have long provided such services to a variety of space stations, including the Salyut series and *Mir*. The Soyuz spacecraft is used to ferry crews, while the Progress is used for supplies. Both designs come from the Apollo era.

The Soyuz and Progress spacecraft are similar in design and both are launched using Soyuz boosters from the Baikonur Cosmodrome in Kazakhstan. The first Soyuz flight was on 23 April 1967 and there have been 94 Soyuz launches in the almost 30 years since. Like Space Shuttle, Soyuz has suffered two fatal accidents, claiming the lives of four cosmonauts. The current TMA version of the Soyuz is capable of seating three crewmembers for flights to the ISS, and unlike the Space Shuttle, uses parachutes to land. A Soyuz capsule is always docked to the ISS to provide an emergency evacuation vehicle.

There have been over 100 Progress logistics flights since the first launch on 20 January 1978. Progress is disposable and burns up during reentry.

In the two photos at right, the Progress M-53 (ISS-18P) logistics spacecraft approaches the aft port of the Zvezda service module on 19 June 2005 as the spacecraft flew 225 miles above Beijing, China. At left, John Phillips works on the dismantled probe-and-cone docking mechanism from the Progress; this mechanism must be removed to gain access to the Progress since it is part of the pressure hatch. (NASA)

At left (from top to bottom) European Space Agency (ESA) astronaut Roberto Vittori of Italy, NASA astronaut John L. Phillips, and Russian Space Agency cosmonaut Sergei K. Krikalev wave goodbye from the base of the Soyuz rocket. The crew launched aboard the Soyuz TMA-6 spacecraft from the Baikonur Cosmodrome in Kazakhstan at daybreak on 15 April 2005. Krikalev and Phillips would spend six months on the ISS, replacing Expedition 10 commander Leroy Chiao and flight engineer Salizhan Sharipov, while Vittori spent eight days on the ISS under a commercial contract between the European Space Agency and the Russian Space Agency, returning to Earth with Chiao and Sharipov on 25 April. Unlike the Americans, the Russians perform almost all launch preparations while the rocket is horizontal in its assembly hangar, and the Soyuz TMA-6 had rolled to its launch pad only two days before the launch. (NASA photos by Bill Ingalls)

The Expedition 11 crew, Sergei Krikalev and John Phillips, landed near Arkalyk, Kazakhstan, on 11 October 2005 after a six-month mission in orbit. Along with space flight participant Greg Olsen, who visited the station for more than a week, Phillips and Krikalev returned to Earth aboard the Soyuz TMA-6 spacecraft. Divots seen in the photo at left were made by the landing jets of the Soyuz spacecraft (background) during its landing. In the center photo, Gagarin Cosmonaut Training Center Deputy Chief Cosmonaut Valery Korzun walks near the TMA-6 capsule at sunrise. At right, Energia technicians remove cargo from TMA-6 after the crew had already egressed. (NASA photos by Bill Ingalls)

LANDING IN CALIFORNIA

STS-114 had been scheduled to land at the Shuttle Landing Facility at the Kennedy Space Center in Florida. Despite staying on-orbit a day longer than originally planned while waiting for the weather in Florida to clear, it was not to be. Flight controllers at the Johnson Space Center finally decided to send *Discovery* to the alternate landing site at Edwards Air Force Base in California. It would be the 50th time a Space Shuttle mission had ended at Edwards.

Due to various restrictions on overflying populated areas, avoiding orbital debris, and other considerations, the landing would take place in the early morning when it was still dark at Edwards. Given the last-minute nature of the decision, hundreds of members of the media, and the astronaut's families, were still waiting at KSC when it was decided to go to Edwards; they would be disappointed.

Astronaut Michael J. "Bloomer" Bloomfield was at Edwards in a Gulfstream Shuttle Training Aircraft, just in case, and performed the normal pre-landing checks of the weather and navigation aids. A small team of KSC employees routinely deploys to Edwards in case a landing is made there, and other workers were quickly on commercial airline flights to augment them.

Entry was normal, although everybody on the ground – and likely in the Orbiter – held their breath longer than normal after the loss of *Columbia* over two years earlier. *Discovery* touched down on Runway 22 at 08:11 a.m. EDT on 9 August 2005, deployed her drag chute, and coasted to a stop. After the crew disembarked and were greeted, workers prepared the Orbiter to be towed to the Mate-Demate Device at Edwards where it was eventually loaded atop a Boeing 747 Shuttle Carrier Aircraft for the trip back to Florida.

Before dawn, members of the media are gathered at the new media facility at Kennedy Space Center's Shuttle Landing Facility to wait for the early morning landing of Discovery. *The landing was eventually diverted to Edwards Air Force Base in California due to weather concerns. The landing occurred at 08:11 EDT on 9 August 2005.* (NASA)

Despite the late notice, the news media arrived at Dryden – not far from Los Angeles – in force. (NASA photo by Tom Tschida)

Discovery landing on the concrete Runway 22 at Edwards AFB. This was the 50th landing at Edwards and the sixth night landing for the Space Shuttle Program. (left: NASA photo by Tony Landis; right: NASA photo by Jim Ross)

Discovery **sitting on the runway at Edwards prior to being towed to the nearby Dryden Flight Research Center.** (NASA by Carla Thomas)

The Crew Transport Vehicle pulls up to Discovery. The aerodynamic flow over the fuselage during entry is easy to see in the this photo by the diagonal line from the leading point of the chine to the front edge of the vertical stabilizer. (NASA photo by Carla Thomas)

Far left and left: **The crew of STS-114 safely on the ground.** (NASA photos by Jim Ross)

Return to Flight – Space Shuttle Discovery

Discovery in the Mate-Demate Device at Dryden. After being deserviced and inspected, the Orbiter will be lifted high enough for the Boeing 747 Shuttle Carrier Aircraft (SCA) to be towed under it. (upper left: NASA photo by Tony Landis; others: NASA photos by Tom Tschida)

Tom Tschida captured a lightning strike in the desert behind the MDD and received an Honorable Mention in Aviation Week & Space Technology's 2005 photo contest. Tom received another honorable mention for the photo at the top of page 95. (NASA photo by Tom Tschida)

Discovery *is towed from the runway to the servicing area at the* **Dryden Flight Research Center.** (NASA photo by Tom Tschida)

Discovery *in the MDD at Dryden. The landing gear is still down, but the entire weight of the vehicle is supported by the cradle attached to the fuselage sides.* (NASA photo by Tony Landis)

Workers at Dryden push the nose landing gear doors closed. This is one of the last steps before the Orbiter is mounted on the SCA. (NASA photo by Tony Landis)

Engineers and technicians examine the Thermal Protection System on the bottom of the Orbiter for damage prior to it being ferried back to the Kennedy Space Center. (NASA photo by Jim Ross)

Technicians prepare to attach the tail cone to Discovery in preparation for her ferry flight to KSC. The tail cone smooths the airflow over the Space Shuttle Main Engines and Orbital Maneuvering System pods, considerably lessening the drag at the back of the Orbiter. NASA has two tail cones, one that was built for the Approach and Landing Tests in the mid-1970s, and another built for Endeavour in the early 1990s that incorporated the modifications necessary to accommodate the Orbiter drag chute compartment. The first tail cone was subsequently modified to a similar configuration. (NASA photo by Tom Tschida)

Technicians inspect one of the aft External Tank attach fittings on Discovery. The same fittings that attach the Orbiter to the ET also are used to mount it on the SCA. (NASA photo by Tony Landis)

Discovery *in the MDD at Dryden. Note the "white room" on the far side that provides environmentally-controlled access to the crew compartment.* (NASA photo by Tom Tschida)

The tail cone is attached, although various gasses and purges are still being supplied to the Orbiter through the hoses connected to the T-0 umbilicals (left of photo) and directly through the vent hole in the tail cone. (NASA photo by Tom Tschida)

Ready to go home. At top, Discovery has been raised in the MDD to allow the SCA to be towed under it. The bottom photo shows the Orbiter being lowered onto the specially-modified Boeing 747 used as a Shuttle Carrier Aircraft (SCA). (NASA photos by Carla Thomas)

Return to Flight – Space Shuttle Discovery

Discovery *heading home to Florida. Lori Losey received the Third Place award in Aviation Week & Space Technology's 2005 photo contest for a different shot taken during* Discovery's *flight.* (NASA photo by Lori Losey)

The SCA and Discovery *lift off from the main runway at Edwards on their way to Florida. This is the first of the Shuttle Carrier Aircraft, registered N905NA, and has been used since the beginning of the program.* (NASA photo by Tony Landis)

BACK IN FLORIDA

Although the Orbiter does not weigh nearly enough to tax the lifting capability of a Boeing 747, the amount of drag it produces has a serious effect on the range and altitude capability of the Shuttle Carrier Aircraft. Because of this, two stops are almost always required to ferry an Orbiter from California to Florida. In the case of STS-114, the stops were at Altus AFB, Oklahoma, and Barksdale AFB, Louisiana. The vehicles stayed an extra day at Barksdale waiting for the weather in Florida to clear. An Air Force KC-135 flew several hours ahead of the SCA to ensure the weather along the path was acceptable. The mated pair finally arrived back at the Shuttle Landing Facility at 10:00 a.m. on 21 August 2005.

The Shuttle Carrier Aircraft touched-down on Runway 15 at the Shuttle Landing Facility (SLF) at 10:00 a.m. EDT on 21 August 2005. Stops were made at Altus AFB, Oklahoma, and Barksdale AFB, Louisiana, where Discovery stayed for two nights because of weather. (NASA)

Discovery sitting atop the SCA just outside the Mate-Demate Device at KSC. A set of airstairs allows the 747 crew to disembark; the Orbiter does not carry a crew during ferry flights. NASA owns two Shuttle Carrier Aircraft – N905NA and N911NA. The winding down of the Space Shuttle Program has allowed 911 to be placed in flyable storage at the Dryden Flight Research Center and all future ferry flights will use 905. (NASA)

After the crew disembarks and the 747 powered-down, the mated pair will be slowly towed into the MDD where the Orbiter will be lifted off the 747. The MDD at KSC is generally similar to the one at Dryden; a less sophisticated version is at the Orbiter manufacturing facility at Palmdale, California. (NASA)

A very similar angle to the photo on page 96, only at KSC instead of Dryden. In the MDD, a horizontal structure mounted at the 80-foot level between two towers controls and guides a large lift beam that attaches to the Orbiter to raise and lower it. (NASA)

A technician checks the crew hatch prior to the Orbiter being demated from the SCA. Note the safety harness to make sure he does not fall off the 80-foot high platform. (NASA)

With the Orbiter securely held by the MDD, the 747 is backed out. The next step is to lower Discovery's landing gear so she can be towed to the Orbiter Processing Facility. (NASA)

Discovery *hanging in the MDD. Note the open ET umbilical well doors under the aft fuselage and the ferry attach point under the forward fuselage. This is where the Orbiter is attached to the Shuttle Carrier Aircraft during the ferry flights, and are the same locations used to mate the Orbiter to the External Tank during launch.* (NASA)

The landing gear has been lowered and Discovery *is almost on the ground. The Orbiter will be towed to one of the Orbiter Processing Facility hangars on her landing gear.* (NASA)

The main cabin in the Shuttle Carrier Aircraft, N905NA. Essentially everything has been removed from the interior, excepting some power and monitoring equipment that connect to the Orbiter and the emergency exit doors along the fuselage sides. (NASA)

The former first-class compartment of the SCA. This is probably one of the few 747s left in service with the original circular staircase to the upper deck. The forward bulkhead has a carpet mural on it depicting a Space Shuttle in flight. (NASA)

The flight deck is a stock 747-100 with a few extra instruments. This 747 was purchased used from American Airlines on 18 July 1974. A second SCA, a Boeing 747-200SR, was purchased in February 1988 and registered N911NA. (NASA)

Discovery poses with N905NA. The 747s are "owned" by the Johnson Space Center and are now kept at the Dryden Flight Research Center in California. The aircraft are not used for other purposes other than proficiency flights by their pilots. (NASA)

Discovery is towed from the Shuttle Landing Facility to Orbiter Processing Facility 3. OPFs 1 and 2 are the buildings in the background in the photo below. Note the post-9/11 security fencing around the OPF. (NASA)

RTF-2 ... STS-121

Before the *Columbia* accident, STS-114 was manifested as an ISS Utilization and Logistics Flight (ULF-1), and the initial post-accident plans called for it to take on the role of Return-to-Flight test mission as well. As 2003 went on, the number of test objectives grew and, as the launch date for STS-114 continued to slip, the logistics needs of ISS increased and it became clear that these objectives could no longer be accomplished in a single flight. In October 2003, NASA essentially split STS-114 into two missions. Stripped of its ISS utilization objectives, STS-114 was redesignated LF-1.

NASA assigns STS numbers in the order manifested, not the order flown. Since STS-115 through STS-120 had already been manifested and crews assigned, the new flight was designated STS-121, ULF-1.1. The flight would be as complex as STS-114, but with a much shorter training schedule and NASA chose to deal with that challenge by reassigning to STS-121 astronauts already assigned to later missions.

In December 2003, NASA announced the first four crewmembers of STS-121. Commander Steven W. Lindsey, pilot Mark E. Kelly, and mission specialist Carlos I. Noriega were reassigned from STS-119, while first-time flyer Michael E. Fossum rounded out the crew. The other three seats were left unassigned in case STS-121 became an ISS crew rotation flight. In July 2004, mission specialist Piers J. Sellers, from STS-120, replaced Noriega due to a temporary medical condition. In November 2004, NASA abandoned the option of performing an ISS crew rotation on STS-121, opting instead to augment the ISS crew from two to three. This opened up two seats for additional shuttle crewmembers, which was necessary because of the increasing workload and complexity of the flight. Mission specialists Lisa M. Nowak and Stephanie D. Wilson were reassigned from STS-118 and STS-120, respectively.

The seventh and final seat on STS-121 was reserved for the third ISS crewmember, originally a Russian slot. In May 2005, Russia sold the seat to ESA, and German astronaut Thomas Reiter was named to the flight. He will remain on ISS after the other STS-121 crewmembers return to Earth, then return to Earth on Soyuz with the other two ISS crewmembers.

The STS-121 patch depicts the Space Shuttle docked with the International Space Station (ISS) in the foreground, overlaying the astronaut symbol with three gold columns and a gold star. The ISS is shown in the configuration that it will be in during the STS-121 mission. The background shows the nighttime Earth with a dawn breaking over the horizon. STS-121, ISS mission ULF1.1, is the final Shuttle Return-to-Flight test mission. This utilization and logistics flight will bring a multipurpose logistics module (MPLM) to the ISS with several thousand pounds of new supplies and experiments. In addition, some new orbital replacement units (ORU) will be delivered and stowed externally on ISS on a special pallet. These ORUs are spares for critical machinery located on the outside of the ISS. During this mission the crew will also carry out testing of TPS inspection and repair hardware, as well as evaluate operational techniques and concepts for conducting on-orbit inspection and repair. (NASA)

Members of the STS-121 crew relax during a training session in July 2005. Note the "STS-114 Discovery" poster in the background and the photos of the two return-to-flight crews on the board behind Thomas Reiter. (NASA)

The official STS-121 crew portrait. From the left are Stephanie D. Wilson, Michael E. Fossum, both mission specialists; Steven W. Lindsey, commander; Piers J. Sellers, mission specialist; Mark E. Kelly, pilot; and Lisa M. Nowak, mission specialist. (NASA)

Steven W. Lindsey

Mark E. Kelly

Michael E. Fossum

Lisa M. Nowak

Carlos I. Noriega

Thomas Reiter

Piers J. Sellers

Stephanie D. Wilson

Discovery in OPF-3 on 28 November 2005. Workers are inspecting Thermal Protection System gap fillers after two were found protruding from the underside of Discovery during STS-114. New installation procedures were developed to ensure the gap fillers stay in place and not pose any hazard on entry. The white strings stretching across the belly of the Orbiter separate prioritized work zones. The work seen here is in zone 1. Over 4,700 gap fillers were replaced on Discovery between STS-114 and STS-121. (NASA)

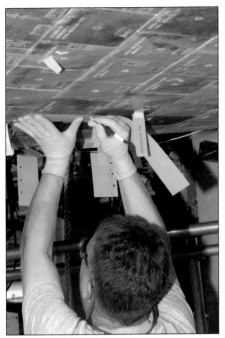

A technician measures, cuts, and installs a strip of gap filler on Discovery in the Orbiter Processing Facility. (NASA)

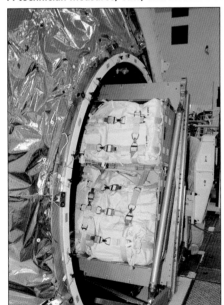

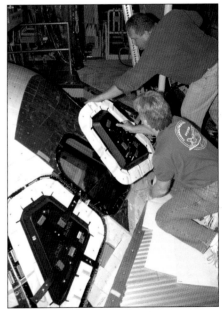

One of the ISS supply racks is installed in the Leonardo MPLM, which will carry more than two tons of equipment and supplies to the ISS. (NASA photo by Jack Pfaller)

Pilot Mark Kelly inspects one of the windows on Discovery. Note the Heads-Up Display (HUD) just in front of Kelly. A similar HUD is located in front of the commander. (NASA)

Technicians in OPF-3 remove the protective cover from a window on Discovery to allow crew members to inspect the window from the cockpit. (NASA)

With the VAB in the background, members of the STS-121 crew pose for photographers after a media conference in February 2006. From the left are Piers Sellers, Mark Kelly, Stephanie Wilson, Lisa Nowak, Steve Lindsey, and Mike Fossum. (NASA photo by Kim Shiflett)

The crew also participated in the Crew Equipment Interface Test (CEIT) in the Space Station Processing Facility. Seen here with Betsy Ahearn (center) are (from left) Mike Fossum, Mark Kelly (obscured), Steve Lindsey, and Piers Sellers. (NASA photo by Kim Shiflett)

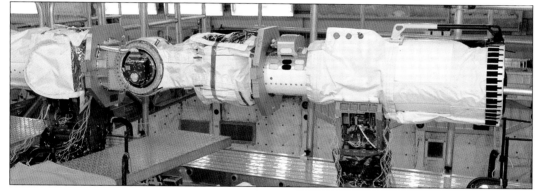

The RMS arm in Atlantis had been equipped with special instrumentation to gather loads data from the second return-to-flight mission, STS-121. When it was decided to use Discovery for STS-121, the arms were switched so that the data could still be gathered on the second flight. (NASA)

One of the fuel cells was removed from Discovery on 5 January 2006 for servicing. The oxygen-hydrogen-powered fuel cells are located under the forward portion of the payload bay and provide all electrical power for the Orbiter. The byproduct from the fuel cells is potable water that is used by the crew while on orbit and also pumped to the International Space Station. (NASA photo by Kim Shiflett)